A House for My Mother

ARCHITECTS BUILD FOR THEIR FAMILIES

A House for My Mother

BETH DUNLOP

PRINCETON ARCHITECTURAL PRESS

New York

Contents

	6	ACKNOWLEDGMENTS
BETH DUNLOP	8	Houses for the Generations
MARK HAMPTON	16	Laura Hampton House TAMPA, FLORIDA 1954
RICHARD MEIER	20	Jerome and Carolyn Meier House ESSEX FALLS, NEW JERSEY 1963
ROBERT VENTURI	24	Vanna Venturi House CHESTNUT HILL, PENNSYLVANIA 1959–1964
CHARLES GWATHMEY	28	Robert and Rosalie Gwathmey House AMAGANSETT, NEW YORK 1963–1967
PETER BOHLIN	32	Eric and Ann Bohlin House WEST CORNWALL, CONNECTICUT 1973–1975
LAURINDA SPEAR AND BERNARDO FORT-BRESCIA	40	Harold and Suzanne Spear House MIAMI SHORES, FLORIDA 1976–1979
STEVEN IZENOUR	48	George and Hilda Izenour House STONY CREEK, THIMBLE ISLAND, CONNECTICUT 1980
MICHAEL FRANKLIN ROSS	52	John and Jean Ross House OLD WESTBURY, LONG ISLAND, NEW YORK 1976–1981
PAUL WESTLAKE	60	John and Carolyn Grima House WARREN, OHIO 1983
MARK SIMON	64	Joan and David Crowell House QUOGUE, NEW YORK 1982–1984
WALTER CHATHAM	72	William Howard and Janet Adams House NEVIS, WEST INDIES 1985
SUZANNE MARTINSON	80	Mel and Avanell Shoar House PUNTA GORDA, FLORIDA 1985
DAVID LESNIAK	88	Len and Jan Lesniak House BAY HEAD, NEW JERSEY 1989
ROBERT KAHN	96	Lawrence and Jane Kahn House SAINT LOUIS, MISSOURI 1988–1990
NATALYE APPEL	104	Tom and Carolyn Caldwell House GALVESTON ISLAND, TEXAS 1990
CHARLES MENEFEE	112	Charles and Lisa Menefee House HURRICANE GAP, NORTH CAROLINA 1990–1992
WHITNEY SANDER	120	John and Gretchen von Storch Swift House BRECKENRIDGE, COLORADO 1992–1994
ROBERT LUCHETTI	128	Lawrence and Petra Luchetti House MIDDLETON, COYOTE VALLEY, CALIFORNIA 1994
PETER AND MARK ANDERSON	136	Charles and Margaret Anderson House SEATTLE, WASHINGTON 1989–1995
CHRIS PARLETTE	144	Bette Parlette and John Fischer House JACKSON, CALIFORNIA 1995
DONNA KACMAR	152	Steve and Diana Kacmar House SPRING BRANCH, TEXAS 1997
ERIC COBB	160	Leonard and Else Cobb House SEATTLE, WASHINGTON 1995–1998
MARK AND JEAN LARSON	168	David and Kathryn Larson House ANNANDALE, MINNESOTA 1998
JOANNA LOMBARD AND DENIS HECTOR	176	Rocci and Anne Lombard House FORT LAUDERDALE, FLORIDA 1998
HENRY MYERBERG	184	Alvin and Louise Myerberg House OWINGS MILLS, MARYLAND 1998
	191	PHOTOGRAPH CREDITS

Acknowledgments

FIRST AND FOREMOST, I WANT TO ADMIT THAT ALTHOUGH I WAS PRESENT AT THE MOMENT THIS book was conceived, the idea actually came from Joe Barnes to whom I owe an enormous debt of gratitude. We were at a luncheon sponsored by the American Institute of Architects Committee on Design at the Walt Disney Co.'s new town of Celebration. The subject came up and Joe, who was seated on my left, said, "Now there's a great book! You should do a book on houses architects have designed for their parents." Mark Simon, who was seated on my right, said, "It's a great idea, and besides, I've done two houses for my mother." I too thought it was a fine idea, and immediately e-mailed my editor, Jan Cigliano, who in turn took it right to her boss, Kevin Lippert, publisher of Princeton Architectural Press. And a book was born.

Then came the search for houses. I must express the greatest gratitude to those who helped in the search. Most of this book was created out of a series of discoveries; one phone call lead to another house, and that to another architect and parents. I am sure that along the way, I have missed architects and houses (three new ones turned up after our design deadline to my great dismay); and I am still wondering about the house that several people recalled as if it were an urban legend (only in this case a rural legend), where parents and children were all architects and designed and built the house together somewhere in Connecticut or Massachusetts or Pennsylvania. No one quite remembers enough about it.

I did already know of a number of architects who had designed houses for their parents, including Robert Venturi and Charles Gwathmey; Joanna Lombard and Denis Hector are friends and colleagues; she and I are co-authoring a forthcoming book on the architecture of Duany and Plater-Zyberk, and Denis and I edited a book together, *Hurricane Hazard Mitigation*. Rocci and Anne Lombard are also longtime friends (and we all are all personally connected in that three of the four Hector and Lombards are godparents to my son). I've known Laurinda Spear and Bernardo Fort-Brescia (and the senior Spears, Harold and Suzanne) for two decades, and have written a book on the work of their firm, Arquitectonica.

I even took my then young son to a birthday party of Laurinda and Bernardo's then young son at the Spear house. Suzanne Martinson designed my kitchen (shortly after finishing her parents' house), and she is married to photographer Steven Brooke, whose work appears on the cover and inside this book. Mark Hampton, too, is a longtime friend, though he is so modest that someone else had to tell me of his mother's house. Mark Simon is not only one of the midwives of the project, but a long-distance friend, and (just to tie things together ever more), he and I both once attended a Committee on Design reception at the Spear house. And others—Peter Bohlin, Walter Chatham, Peter Dominick—are among the architects I've been privileged to know over the years.

Not everyone was known to me, however. I want to thank every one of the architects and their parents who are in this book, or who I contacted; I have been very privileged to meet up with those whose work is depicted here; our numerous conversations have been both enjoyable and enriching. I thank the many associates in the many architectural offices, who put together packages of slides and drawings and the parents who dug into old photo albums. I also want to thank those who led me to these architects, including: Carl Abbott, Jay Baker, Tom Beeby, Tom Conner, Steven Erhlich, Gail Foerster, Lisa Green, Graham Gund, Jim Jennings, John Izenour, Linda Myers, Sheri Olson, Jerry Pignolet, Tom Sansone, Mack Scogin, Schaeffer Somers, Karen Stein, Robert A.M. Stern, Kate Stirling, Ted Tanaka, and Dennis Wilhelm. Given the subject of this book, I'd be remiss not to acknowledge my parents: my late father Craig Dunlop, who had his whole family in hard hats and on construction sites while others were taking Sunday drives to the country, and my mother, Elinor Dunlop, whose aesthetic sensibilities and writing talents certainly shaped my future. And of course, last but never least, I thank my husband, Bill Farkas, and son, Adam Farkas, for their support and for putting up with me while I finish a book.

Richard Rogers, with his first wife Su Rogers, designed this house for his parents in 1968–1969.

Houses for the Generations

BETH DUNLOP

THE HOUSES ARCHITECTS DESIGN FOR THEIR PARENTS ARE PLIED WITH MANY LAYERS OF MEANING, even if on the surface they seem to be simply houses. Large or small, modernist or historically referential, experimental or prudent—they are not, even possibly, objective works of architecture. They are personal, in one way or another, and they are heartfelt. And it is these very qualities that set the houses in this book apart from all others, even the houses that architects design for themselves.

And inevitably so: the relationship of parent and child is like no other, at once basic and complex, propelled by commonalties and differences. Think about it. Parents bring children into the world, clothe and feed them, nurture and educate them, and for the first decade or so they are one with them. Then they break away, forging their own lives in the world they will inhabit for decades to come. Yet parents remain parents forever, authority figures and purveyors of wisdom. To design a house for a parent is to tip the balance between authority and deference. Even those parents who become complete patrons, giving their designer offspring full artistic license and complete architectural autonomy, become the takers and not the givers. The parent-clients represented here range (to hear their offspring tell it) from too-easy-to-please to difficult-to-read to impossible-to-please. Represented in the following pages are parents-as-patrons, parents-as-clients, and—in the words of Henry Myerberg—"parents-as-parents."

Psychologists tell us that it is during late childhood and adolescence that our children become "critics," appraising and evaluating all that is around them and choosing to adopt or adapt what seems appropriate to their own lives. To listen to the stories of the twenty-five architects in these pages, we can see how the child-as-critic takes shape; many drew inspiration for their work by the act of embracing and rejecting, keeping and letting go. Whether children turn away from their parents or reaffirm their interests and habits, they ultimately form their own lives apart from them. And then, children mature, marry, become parents themselves, and the cycle repeats. Perhaps it is at this point, either in the life cycle or in age, that children realize there are few people in their lives they know so well and yet so little. Who among us hasn't been surprised by a late-in-life (or at least later) disclosure by one or both parents of an unfulfilled ambition, or a long-held dream?

I began this book with the idea that, given the complexities of the parent-child relationship and given the ties that bind us to our families, the houses architects design for their parents would lead to a greater understanding of the meaning and nature of home. Usually, architects design houses, not homes: a home is a social place created by its inhabitants. There is an enormous difference in meaning between the two words, home and house; home is personal, with all the implications of domesticity and intimacy, while house is simply a physical envelope. It is neutral—wood or steel or stone or concrete or glass.

Indeed, the houses architects designed for their parents impart notions about comfort, care, sustenance, memory, history, tradition—even those that are emphatic modernist exercises. In many cases, architects are replacing a childhood home, one with deep and personal connections to the past. They faced the challenge of making a new space yet linking it in some way to entrenched memories and customs of the family, sometimes subtly and sometimes explicitly. Some of the houses shown here incorporate tangible pieces of the past. Mark and Jean Larson, for example, reused the timber from the family's old Minnesota lake house in the new one, and Mark and Peter Anderson centrally placed the family heirloom, a Norwegian krumkakke iron (brought across the Atlantic by their great-great-grandmother) in the kitchen of their parents' house on the shores of Puget Sound.

More often, the connections were not so much with the family's immediate past but with a somehow vaster history. Most of the houses shown here are linked to the regional landscape or to the vernacular architecture to be found nearby. In such cases as the house designed by Joanna Lombard and Denis Hector for her parents (and his in-laws), or the house designed by Henry Myerberg for his parents, the connections to history are straightforward. The architects have made conscious choices to reflect stylistic references from historic buildings nearby, but not to copy. Others, such as Robert Kahn's suburban St. Louis house, is intended to seem house-like, to reflect its own time and all time, at least in domestic suburban America.

Certainly, there was much to learn. Peter and Mark Anderson, for example, realized they had taken for granted much of what they thought they knew about their parents and the family, "but now were asked to make these into a built structure." And yet, there is also a rare intimacy to this. Charles Menefee points out that "all the archispeak goes away and instead you are thinking about such things as: 'Where are we going to put the silverware? Where does the rum go? Who's going to vacuum? Where do the sheets go?' And yet you still want to have it be beautiful."

Although the houses shown here are all new, there are indeed instructive examples of ways in which architects have adapted existing houses, with an eye to continuity and change. Such was the case of Peter Dominick's renovation of a half-century old family house in the suburbs of Denver. Dominick's father—an attorney who later became a United States Senator and a pioneering environmentalist—had moved his family to Denver just after World War II and bought a large swath of farmland, actually "a single dirt road running through vast wheat fields." There, the prominent local architect Burnham Hoyt designed the "Igloo House," a two-bedroom frame-and-clapboard dwelling, for Dominick's grandfather. Later, the Igloo House became the family's home away from Washington, "a wonderful little home, comfortable, informal and on a beautiful site with a spectacular view of the Rockies," says Peter Dominick.

In 1974, the senior Dominicks (he was then U. S. Ambassador to Switzerland and was afflicted with multiple sclerosis and wheelchair-bound) asked their son to retrofit the Igloo House. It was Dominick's first commission. He undertook it with an eye to retaining the intent of Hoyt's original design, yet with the mandate to accommodate a parent in failing health. "I rented a wheelchair and tried to understand what were handicap issues, discovering among other things that circulation paths must be simple, doorways wide enough, and changes in elevation must be kept to a minimum."

The combined issues of aging and infirmity are very real factors that most children resist facing, generally and when specifically designing a house for parents. Like Dominick, Henry Myerberg designed for a parent afflicted with multiple sclerosis. In several of the houses, architects tacitly chose to allow for future infirmities—for the quite practical reason that their parents were approaching their 60s and 70s and beyond—and made hallways and doorways wide enough for handicapped access. Donna Kacmar chose to use a single connecting corridor to link all rooms, and allow for the eventuality of a wheelchair; Joanna Lombard and Denis Hector simply made the doorways three feet wide.

AFFORDABLE INNOVATIONS

There are other ways in which the houses shown here are instructive, offering pragmatic, cost-observant solutions to tricky problems. There are many lessons to be learned: in the conservation of energy and space without a loss of form or function; in the connecting of architecture and garden; in the use of everyday materials as if they were elegant and expensive ones, (such as steel tubing for a handrail and concrete slabs for finished flooring).

A number of the houses on these pages are in country and look out onto vast, expansive landscapes. Others, however, have been built on limited pieces of land; these houses are especially instructive in making the most of small lots, capturing views or providing lush gardens—nurture and nature at once.

Some of the houses shown here are big; most of them are not. They are designed for couples whose families are grown and gone, not for those who are still growing; yet they are also houses for children and grandchildren to return to. While the largest of them provide places for intimacy, the smallest still accommodate visitors gracefully.

CREATIVE EYES, ARTISTIC ROOTS

If these houses did not always suggest easy generalizations, the stories behind them did indeed offer real insights, some architectural, but more of them personal. I learned more than I ever had before about the kinds of homes that produce architects, enough to fill several equations. Some designers grew up in highly artistic, aesthetically attuned households; others did not but found their way anyway to the ideas of commodity, firmness, and light.

Those of us who are parents know how early that awareness of the designed environment can emerge. My teenaged son, who aspires to write and direct films rather than design buildings (or comment on them in critical essays), displayed an uncanny interest in modernism early on. He lived then and still does in an eclectic 1930s Miami Beach house—part Southwestern, part California Spanish, part Mediterranean Revival, part Art Deco—filled with his mother's collections of 1930s art pottery, primitive painted furniture, and treasures from junk shops and estate sales. At one point (he was five or six), his father and I were planning to redo his bedroom with a funky cowboy motif, but he rebelled, insisting on black and white with touches of red and blue, asking for a Rietveld chair (which he did not get) and a most reductive geometric print for his bedspreads (which he did get). By now his mostly modernist room has evolved into something more like the rest of the house: he sleeps in his great-grandfather's spindle bed, has a Turkish rug on the floor, colorful Guatemalan fabric on a sofa, and posters for *Casablanca* and *Rebel Without a Cause* (among other films) on the walls. Still, his visual sensibilities emerged early and remain well honed: to this day he dreams of the $800 poster for Fritz Lang's *Metropolis* that he can't afford.

I offer this story because there is a point of self-realization there. My child, most children—no matter how many remarkable genetic similarities a parent does or wants to see—are always going to view the world through his or her own eyes, convinced that he or she is somehow seeing a world more profound, more urgent, more lucid perhaps than that of their parents. And certainly this was unstated in the stories are told here, because that is the reality of the creative soul. There were some fluky coincidences. In one single day, for example, both Robert Kahn and Charles Menefee told me they had grown up in modern houses their parents had commissioned from two regionally renowned followers of Frank Lloyd Wright. Two others (Henry Myerberg and David Lesniak) described their fascination as children with the construction process as their family homes were built or rebuilt. Chris Parlette remembers as a young teenager walking around the San Francisco suburb where he lived simply wondering how things could be so repetitive, so ugly.

Patterns surfaced: in this group are several designers of Scandinavian descent (Martinson, Anderson and Anderson, Larson), and each one, in turn, talked of the Scandinavian aesthetic that informs their designs. Many of the architects in this book have a parent who is an artist (and a number also have artist siblings): Charles Gwathmey is the son of the well-known muralist and painter, Robert Gwathmey; his photographer-mother Rosalie achieved perhaps less recognition. Eric Cobb, Robert Luchetti, Michael Franklin Ross, and Whitney Sander all have an artist parent. Suzanne Martinson's parents are boatbuilders. Paul Westlake was schooled in architecture by his uncle Merle Westlake, a homebuilder, and his parents also took him to see many important works of design. Donna Kacmar's parents wanted to be architects but became an engineer and an urban planner. Still others—Robert Venturi, Richard Meier, Robert Kahn, Henry Myerberg—speak of their parents' art collections; certainly a childhood surrounded by works of art refines the eye. And much later, these architects would design houses to accommodate the pieces they came to love as children.

Indeed as Venturi talks of how the house he designed for his mother evolved—a house that unlike Gwathmey's or Meier's signaled a shift not just for one architect but ultimately for many—he realized that he needed to design in a particular way to let his mother be at home with her furniture, objects, and antiques, which she had gathered over almost three decades. For Venturi, that meant a return to a more symbolic and metaphoric architecture, one that, in his words, was about shelter rather than enclosure.

SHELTERING WALLS

In some ways the notion of shelter is still a radical idea in architecture. Yet the houses shown here are indeed shelters; they embrace their occupants and offer places for family and friends to convene, whether to fulfill customs or by chance. Even the most abstract of these houses is not an object for a frozen moment in time but a house that will host Christmas celebrations, christenings, wedding receptions. These, in the words of Joanna Lombard, "restore the concept of a house as a generational place." This is an important idea, and one that has frequently been lost in a mobile society. Some of the houses designed here were created at a distance—for families that were hours or days apart—but all were made with an eye to the home as a gathering place. It is telling, too, that of the 27 houses shown here, houses designed over the course of more than four decades, only five no longer belong to the families who created them; even in these cases, the architects and their families remain closely tied to them. The oldest, Mark Hampton's 1954 house in Tampa, is still family owned and occupied. Likewise, Charles Gwathmey's mother, Rosalie Gwathmey, celebrated her 90th birthday in 1998 in the Amagansett Beach house her son built for her in 1967.

American architects designed all the houses in this book. Yet the act of designing for a parent is not unique to our generation or to a specific culture or country. In 1918, Alvar Aalto, then just 20, renovated a cottage in Alajarvi, Finland, for his parents; though his first work, it is not commemorated in any way. Neither drawings nor photographs of it seem to remain.

Le Corbusier built a house for his parents on the banks of Lake Geneva in Switzerland, and published it in a charming small book, *Une Petite Maison.* It was a long, low-slung house made of concrete, which he described this way: "The height of the house is two-and-a-half meters (the regulation minimum). It resembles a long box lying on the ground. The rising sun is caught at one end by a slanting skylight, and for the rest of the day it passes on its circuit in front of the house. Sun, space and greenness—what more could be wanted?" The house was built in 1923 and 1924; his father lived in it only one year, but his mother remained for several decades and celebrated her 91st birthday there in 1951. It was a controversial house; Corbusier recounts that after it was completed, a neighboring municipal council met and voted that such houses were crimes against nature and thus prohibited.

More recently, in 1968 and 1969, British architect Richard Rogers designed, with Su Rogers then his wife, a house for his parents in Wimbledon, on a long and narrow wooded plot of land across from the Common. It is a steel and glass house, divided in two parts—a pottery studio and separate flat near the road and the main house set into the trees behind. It is a splendidly simple house—lucid and elegant, timeless in style, though of its time. And indeed these qualities emerge so clearly in *A House for My Mother:* even the oldest of the houses have transcended their own time; they are rooted in an understanding of how people live and occupy a house that makes them seem fresh still, not dated.

This brings us full circle, back to the idea of place. It is through the houses we live in that we first derive a sense of place, and continue to do so over the years. To be sure, there are examples here of what might be considered placeless houses—the formalistic and modernist houses by Richard Meier, Charles Gwathmey, Peter Bohlin, Michael Franklin Ross— houses that relate more to a specific site than to a larger geographic or historic context. These are the exceptions, albeit well-known exceptions, rather than the rule. The works shown on these pages offer a range of approaches to the contexts of time and place: some of them are about the past; others about the future, and a majority are positioned in a specific place rather than a particular time, designed to embrace the history, the conventions, or the vernacular of a region. And that, in a way, provides the philosophical underpinning of the book. Even in our very mobile society there are connections that bind us—family, history, geography—and these can be expressed in architecture. It is heartening to see this, to see families rooted and together, a condition enhanced by architecture fulfilling its historic ceremonial role as refuge and gathering place. Houses can be homes.

Joanna Lombard's and Denis Hector's design for Rocci and Anne Lombard house, Fort Lauderdale, Florida, 1998

Laura Hampton's house, tucked into the landscape beneath maturing oak trees

<small>MARK HAMPTON</small>

Laura Hampton House

<small>TAMPA, FLORIDA 1954</small>

THIS WAS THE SECOND AND THE SMALLER OF TWO HOUSES MARK HAMPTON DESIGNED FOR HIS mother, Laura Hampton. Both houses—this one is still in the family—are in Tampa. It was a design predicated on the dappled sunlight and the elegant shade of the Southern live oak. The trees on the site were young in 1954. Today, the house is all but obscured by the sprawling branches of fully mature oaks.

Back in 1949 Laura Hampton had moved into the first house her son had designed, a work Hampton completed right after he graduated from Georgia Tech. It was a big house, however, and on land devoid of trees. Soon she decided that the house was too big, and she longed for one more compact and on a shadier site. An avid gardener, Laura Hampton was known for her azaleas and camellias—and for her trademark arrangements that always included a sprig from an oak tree. Too, because azaleas and camellias are acid-loving plants, Laura Hampton was constantly in search of leaves with which to pack the ground.

Thus, when Mark Hampton found the site for this house in Tampa's genteel Beach Park district, he was drawn to it by the almost whimsical idea that his mother would no longer have to scrounge oak leaves from friends and neighbors. It was also a beautiful piece of property. In the 1950s, Florida offered fertile ground—for trees and for young mod-

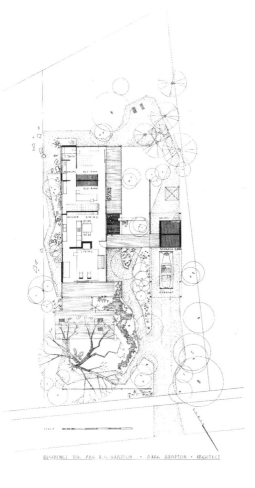

Plan of house shows its placement in the landscape.

ernists exploring the relationships of architecture and nature. Paul Rudolph had already gone to work in Sarasota, creating some of his finest and most thoughtful pieces there, but he was not alone. Hampton, who still lives and practices in Miami, was among the early talented modernists to design houses that were at once sensitive to their surroundings and formalistic about their architecture.

Air-conditioning was not preponderant in the early 1950s, which meant that houses in Florida had to rely more on shade and cross-ventilation than on mechanical systems, so Hampton created a house that is low to the ground and nestled under the trees. It is built of white brick with wooden jalousies covering window openings.

Because the largest tree was out front, Hampton brought the living room and outdoor terraces out front also. Other rooms unfold behind it—the kitchen, dining room, and two bedrooms. At one side of the lot is a carport, along with laundry and storage rooms; a white-brick walkway leads from there into the house, a long and narrow rectangle. Two sides of the house are lined with terraces. Both the overhanging flat roofs and the abundant trees provide shade. And, Hampton recalls, his mother never felt closed in, even though the house was small. "She would often say that at friends' houses, she'd feel claustrophobic," he says. "She liked living in a glass house."

Each room, including the kitchen, is connected to the view, allowing for both sunlight and breezes.

RIGHT **Entrance to the house along a covered walkway**

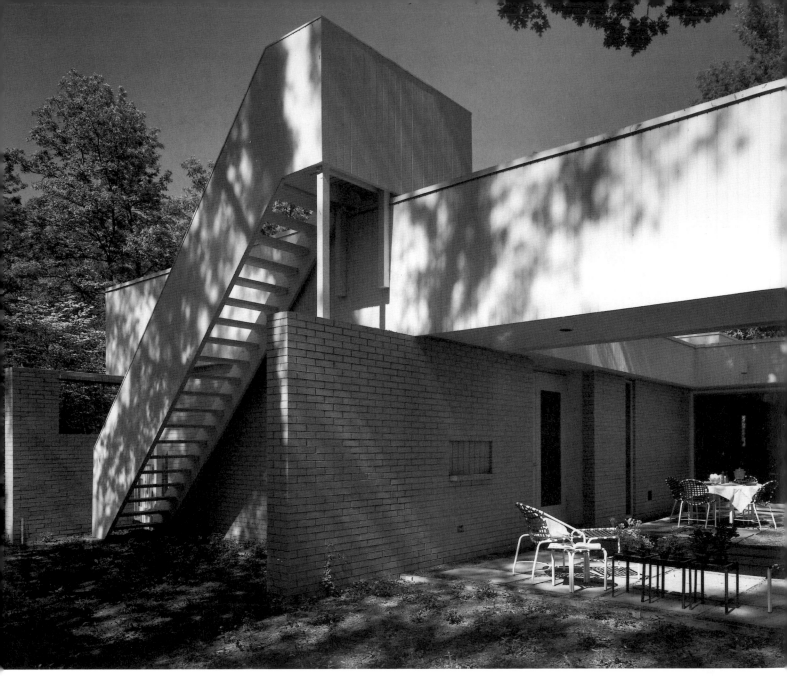

Richard Meier describes his design as "a Miesian brick house under a Frank Lloyd Wright roof."

RICHARD MEIER

Jerome and Carolyn Meier House

ESSEX FALLS, NEW JERSEY 1963

RICHARD MEIER GREW UP IN A THREE-STORY "PSEUDO-COLONIAL" HOUSE IN NEW JERSEY. BY THE time he had opened his own architectural practice—after working for several other architect's firms—his parents were ready to move to a smaller, simpler house. Two of Jerome and Carolyn Meier's three sons were grown and gone, and the third was soon to head off to college.

The Meiers selected a heavily wooded one-acre suburban tract close by the house they had long lived in. They asked their son Richard to design a house on a single floor, "one that was easier to live in and easier to maintain," Meier says. It was not the first project he had done on his own; Meier had already completed a small beach house in Fire Island and renovated a larger house in New Jersey. A singular oak tree, large and imposing, stood on the site and guided the house's placement. Meier designed the house to preserve most of the trees and to maximize the views. Though the lot was just one acre, it opened onto a golf course to afford a much longer view through the trees and onto the fairways.

The house is made of brick, inside and out, and covered by a large overhanging wooden roof. Meier calls it "a Miesian brick house under a Frank Lloyd Wright roof." The roof actually houses a garden and overlooks a courtyard, which is set off-center to give the dining room and the master bedroom access to a private outdoor space. The master bedroom and living room are set on one side of the house, while the kitchen and two guest bedrooms are at the other. Both the courtyard and the curving brick walls that extend beyond the corners were designed to "protect and shape the views" and to allow for privacy. Conversely, skylights and clerestory windows bring the outside into the house. "Sunlight and shadows inundate the interior," says Meier, "producing a sense of space and quietude."

Although his parents, he remembers, had strong opinions about what they liked and wanted in a house, they also gave him rather free reign. "They were courageous," Meier says. At one point they told him they were willing to buy almost all new furniture, more fitting with the house. Thus encouraged, Meier designed a dining table and built-in sofas for them, and filled the rest of the house with chairs designed by Mies van der Rohe and Eero Saarinen and couches by Florence Knoll. The artwork on the walls included paintings by Josef Albers and by Meier himself. "And it was what they wanted," Meier says. "They were great clients."

Over the years, Jerome and Carolyn Meier relished the house. "My mother always said everything was perfect, except for one thing—there weren't enough closets," says Meier. Jerome Meier is no longer living. Carolyn Meier now divides her time between apartments in New Jersey and Boca Raton, Florida. "They loved the freedom. They loved the transparency," says Richard Meier.

Carolyn Meier, left, with son Richard, when he received the AIA Gold Medal.

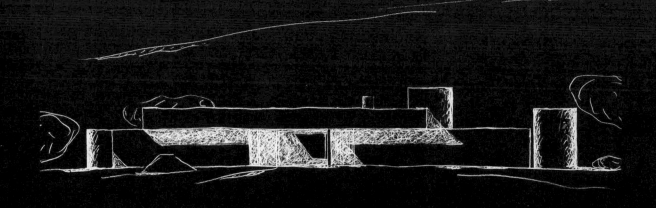

WEST ELEVATION

RESIDENCE FOR MR AND MRS WEBB
ESSEX FELLS   NEW JERSEY
RICHARD MEIER   ARCHITECT

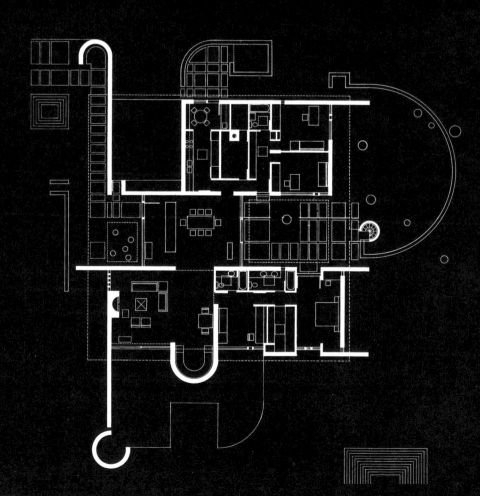

ABOVE **The house is tucked into the trees in its suburban setting.**

BELOW RIGHT **The Meier family selected furniture fitting with the house's modernist design.**

LEFT **A sketched elevation and a plan for what was Meier's second built work.**

Vanna Venturi in front of the house that launched her son's career

ROBERT VENTURI AND DENISE SCOTT BROWN
Vanna Venturi House

CHESTNUT HILL, PENNSYLVANIA 1959–1964

> This building recognizes complexities and contradictions: it is both complex and
> simple, open and closed, big and little; some of its elements are good on one level
> and bad on another—the order and the circumstantial elements of this house in
> particular. It achieves the difficult unity of a medium number of diverse parts rather
> than the easy unity of few or many motifs.
>
> —ROBERT VENTURI, writing in *Complexity and Contradiction in Architecture*, 1966

Robert Venturi began designing the house for his mother when he was a single, unmarried man and completed it during his courtship with Denise Scott Brown. It is arguably the most renowned house designed for a parent in recent times. It was the subject of a 1988 exhibition at the Museum of Modern Art in New York City and a book, *Mother's House*, edited by Frederick Schwartz. In its use of classical and vernacular elements, and its embrace of architectural iconography, it set the stage for a long and important career. Years later, Venturi looked back at the house and commented that "what seemed extraordinary then seems ordinary now—and vice versa."

Vanna Venturi had bought three-quarters of an acre in the Philadelphia suburb of Chestnut Hill in 1959, after the death of her husband, Robert Venturi Sr. It was a peculiarly configured lot across the street from Louis Kahn's Esherick House. Although her son by then had worked for Oscar Stonorov, Eero Saarinen, and Kahn, and had received the prestigious Rome Prize, he had not at that point designed a building of his own. This would be his first architectural commission (though he spent so long designing it that it became his second built work).

Vanna Venturi, who died in 1975, did not want an ostentatious house; she did not want an expensive house; and she did not need a garage because she didn't drive. Beyond these minimal requests, she made no demands, giving her son the freedom to explore, experiment, and to start over as he wished. In the course of the six years of design and construction, Venturi created six different schemes for the house, with scale models that are in the permanent collection of the Museum of Modern Art. The early designs had a square plan, which ultimately became a rectangle. Later, Venturi says, the house "started out more like Kahn" but that his own intuition eventually "took control of my hand." The result was a house that was at once "modern and not modern."

The house uses abstracted iconography to express architectural ideas.

Ultimately, it is a complex house—but one in which simplified elements are given an outsized scale. The front façade is symmetrical in form, more or less; the symmetry is skewed by the placement of such elements as the windows and the chimney. For example, one side of the enormous split gable has two square windows, a larger mullioned one and a smaller one; the other side has a horizontal window composed of five connected squares. The chimney rises behind the gable, set off center. The door is centered and sits under an applied ornamental fragment of a circle.

A key to the design was accommodating the furniture Vanna Venturi had collected over the years.

ROBERT VENTURI AND DENISE SCOTT-BROWN

On the façade, Venturi applies conventional house elements unconventionally, which emphasizes the classical and domestic symbolism of the house. The combination of the classical and the domestic has remained central to Venturi's architectural philosophy through the years. His work has involved both sign and symbol, and this house is no exception. "With its gable roof, central door, ordinary windows and chimney, it looked like an elemental house, like a child's drawing of a house," Venturi reflected in an essay written 25 years after the house was completed.

Inside the house, the elements are also familiar and unfamiliar, "complex," says Venturi, "in both shapes and relationships." Again, there is symmetry and distorted symmetry; the two dominant elements of the first floor—the fireplace and the chimney—"compete with each other for a central position." Venturi designed an interior to be welcoming to his mother's "old furniture," circa 1925 pieces and some antiques, which was daring for its traditionalism in an era of pure and modern interiors.

When it was completed in 1964, Robert Venturi painted the exterior a taupe gray. Vanna Venturi and her son moved in on April 1st of that year. Two years later, he painted it green (a response to a comment from Marcel Breuer that green was the color of nature and therefore should never be used on buildings) and married Scott Brown. The three lived in the house for several months, until Venturi and Scott Brown moved to an apartment in Center City Philadelphia. In 1973, Agatha and Thomas Hughes, a potter and a professor, bought Vanna Venturi's house, and have lived there now for over a quarter-century.

First and second floor
plans of the house

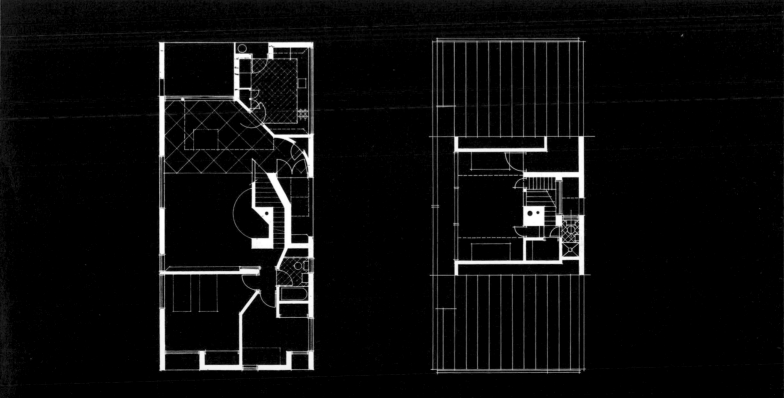

The main house, foreground, was built first, then the studio.

CHARLES GWATHMEY

Robert and Rosalie Gwathmey House

AMAGANSETT, NEW YORK 1963–1967

CHARLES GWATHMEY GREW UP WITH A PAINTER FATHER, AND A PHOTOGRAPHER MOTHER. HIS aesthetic sensibilities were honed early. As a child he would watch Robert Gwathmey paint, or spend evenings with Rosalie Gwathmey as she worked in her darkroom. "I'm sure it all had a subconscious or even direct impact on my being a modernist, and being a Cubist, and understanding shapes and forms in a way that was less representational," says Gwathmey. And even today, the architect's work centers on the ideas of art—of the Cubist perception of space, of the modernist painter's use of color. This house, designed just two years after he received his architectural degree from Yale University, foreshadows such continuing preoccupations as "transparency, perceptual and literal extension, and volumetric interpenetration," he explains.

Gwathmey was working in Edward Larrabee Barnes' architectural office when his parents asked him to design the house. They had located a piece of land on Long Island, an empty field fronting the ocean and surrounded by undeveloped land that was inevitably destined for development. Robert Gwathmey, who died in 1979, was a widely respected painter known for social realism. Renowned in her own right, Rosalie Gwathmey was a founding member of the New York Photo League and photographed many of the black sharecroppers and Southern townscapes that became the basis of her husband's paintings. She celebrated her 90th birthday in 1998—in the Amagansett house.

At the time of the commission, Robert and Rosalie Gwathmey told their son, "Build it as if it was for you, but you are us." It was not as tricky a mandate as it might sound. Gwathmey's father was a modernist with a love for modern architecture; he was a painter whose work was "highly delineated, both in terms of shapes and color," Gwathmey believes.

Gwathmey supervised all the workmanship on the house to ensure that it was well crafted.

The young Gwathmey took the plunge: he left his job, took a teaching post at Pratt Institute, and began focusing on the design and construction of the house. "It was part of my ambition, and part of my impatience, but I believed in it," he says. "And everyone thought I was crazy." It was a chance that paid out, of course. "The only way to both grow and learn and to also make your statement is to take the risk. And of course, the risk embodies the possibility of failure, but that's the only way you know if you can do it or not."

The house, with 1,200 square feet including living/dining space, a kitchen, a master bedroom/studio, two guest bedrooms, and a workroom, was designed and built in 1966 as a summer residence. A year later, Robert and Rosalie Gwathmey decided to move there permanently. Gwathmey designed a second, smaller structure (480 square feet), to create an additional guestroom and a painting studio for his father, who had taught at Cooper Union yet had always painted at home.

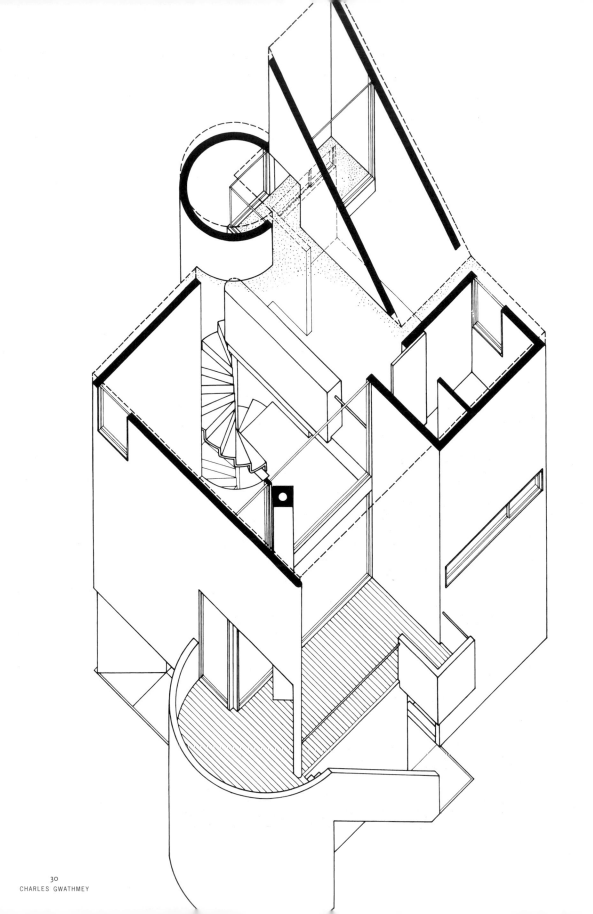

Both buildings are clad in cedar siding, left to fade over the years, inside and out. The intent was to make them seem carved from a solid volume rather than assembled as pieces put together or a series of planes. Indeed, as Gwathmey was designing, it became clear the architect would become the contractor. He sought out others to build it, but the contractors he talked to "had never seen cedar siding and curves." The bids were staggering. "I decided to build it myself," Charles Gwathmey remembers.

Gwathmey spent five days a week at the site. He hired all the subcontractors and supervised the entire job. It was an "unbelievable lesson," he says today, one in which he learned the full breadth of architecture. Though the main house is a small footprint and 30,000 cubic feet of space, its organization is vertical rather than horizontal, a design that was especially bold when houses tended to sprawl out over their sites.

In the main structure, guest rooms and workroom make up the first floor, along with a covered terrace. Living, cooking, and eating spaces occupy the second floor, and the master bedroom is on the third, which is actually a balcony overlooking the two-story living room. Gwathmey placed the house's primary spaces high for one pragmatic reason—to maintain a sense of privacy—and one poetic reason—to evoke the tradition of the rural "raised

house." The smaller studio sits at a 45-degree angle to the original house, but it reflects the house's design. Gwathmey wanted to establish "a perceptual dynamic of corner versus facade." The main house is fully "anchored," he explains, while the studio is more "precarious . . . almost in motion." The house set the standard for Gwathmey's future designs. "It is still," he says, "the very essence of my work. It has a density and a durability and a kind of irrefutability for me. It was clearly a defining moment." And as for his parents, "I think I interpreted their vision well," Charles Gwathmey says. "My mother says she's never going to leave this house."

LEFT **An axonometric view of the Robert and Rosalie Gwathmey residence**

Eric and Ann Bohlin House

WEST CORNWALL, CONNECTICUT 1973–1975

PETER BOHLIN DESIGNED TWO HOUSES FOR HIS PARENTS, NOT QUITE A DECADE APART. THE second house, which was published widely, says Bohlin, "is the more famous of the two. It came at a critical juncture in my career." The house is still in the family, still used as a summer retreat. Yet it is the first house, long since sold, that Bohlin believes his parents— especially his mother—most cherished. "I never figured out why but I think it had to do with light. I think my mom really responded to it. . . . One thing about my mom is that she always loved the sun, and this really reaches out to the sun."

The first house was in Pennsylvania, where the Bohlin family had eventually settled after Eric Bohlin's career as a pencil company executive had taken them there; they had lived in New York and Connecticut, as well. Bohlin was just starting out. "Such houses as these often come very early in an architect's career," says Peter Bohlin of the first of two houses he designed for his parents, "and they come from parents believing in their children. After all, in those days, who else would trust us?" This house derives its design directly from his years at Cranbrook. It was his first independent commission, yet one he says that "offers all sorts of antecedents for our later work."

The house was built on a hilly wooded site in northeastern Pennsylvania on land with a pond and unspoiled views into the pine and hardwood forests and the mountains beyond. The senior Bohlins asked that it open up to the view and allow as much sunlight as possible inside but still afford a sense of privacy. The Bohlins further wished that the house feel intimate to a couple whose children were grown and gone and yet accommodate large gatherings of family and friends. Though in the woods, this was not a rustic house, but rather more sophisticated, clad in wood and furnished with its share of Cranbrook-pedigreed modern furniture (from Eero Saarinen and Florence Knoll, among others) and a large-scale hanging by Bohlin's sister, Nancy Merritt. Typical of its times, it had a sunken "conversation pit" in front of the fireplace, though this one relied on built-in furniture and a spare, architectonic fireplace.

Bohlin designed the living portion of the house on a lower plateau, between the pine grove to the north and the pond to the south. In this, he provides both privacy and a sense of discovery within the house. "You would enter into

LEFT
The house is delicately inserted amid trees.

BELOW
Bohlin's work always involves a processional pathway.

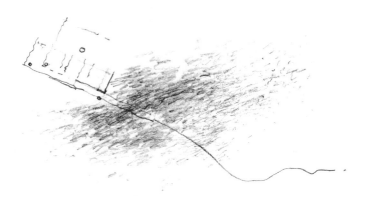

the house and then discover the pond and the sun," says Bohlin. "I've always felt that one of the keys to architecture is how you experience a house as you move through it." To maximize the amount of light, the circulation follows the curved wall of north end of the house, to provide both privacy and to shelter the house from winter winds. The living spaces open east, west, and south. "Always there has been the one thread in our work, getting from here to there, revealing the nature of places, layers in building."

As Eric and Ann Bohlin approached retirement age, they asked their son to design another house for them, this one a summer house in Connecticut where they would live for about half the year. It did not need to be grand, but rather a house in sync with nature. The design does that in almost every way possible to the point that the outdoor decks wrap around existing trees.

The earlier Bohlin house was in rural Pennsylvania in a pine grove at the edge of a forest.

The Bohlin family had lived on the land where this house was built during Peter's childhood. Eventually his parents sold off all but 18 acres. Oddly, back in the 1940s and 1950s, the town hermit had lived on a one-room house on almost exactly where Peter Bohlin was later to build for his parents. The hermit died and his house simply disappeared; local lore holds that it was carried off in pieces by the hermit's relatives.

As is true in all of Bohlin's work, the approach and processional become as much a part of the architecture as the design itself. In this case, the house is reached from the southwest. "Its position is a potent one in the landscape," says Bohlin. "You come through a dark evergreen forest and that becomes a sunny deciduous forest. The path twists through the forest, and there on a sudden shift in the landscape is the building."

Even then, the house doesn't announce itself grandly. "At the time, I was interested in making architecture in which I didn't seem to have tried too hard, or rather the architecture didn't seem to have tried too hard. . . ." The house is stained a dark green, and passage through it is marked by a sequence of red landmarks. The first is a red column, which marks a stair leading to a red door and into the house where two more red columns rise up. The three red columns extend from the ground up through the body of the house; they are the only columns to penetrate the interior space. Others are for reinforcement rather than spatial continuity, to lift the house off the rocky terrain.

The house is long and narrow, only 16 feet wide, in fact. Its linear quality is reinforced by the approach—path becomes bridge; bridge becomes covered breezeway; breezeway unfolds into vestibule. From there the house splits into two wings—one housing the master bedroom and kitchen below and a study and guest bedroom above, the other opening onto a two-story living room. Bohlin chose a vast industrial multi-paned window to form two of the living room walls. "Rather large sheets of glass would have been overpowering," Bohlin says. "This is more of a tapestry with a delicacy to it. It's kind of a delicate net around the space." The glass is tinted slightly gray.

Throughout the house, materials are rather rugged, starting with the stained cedar. The roof is a parallelogram of corrugated aluminum. Bohlin relied on built-in furniture for both simplicity and artistry. A single Noguchi lamp sits at the nexus of the industrial window. "There is a very simple set of thoughts at work," says Bohlin. "I wanted to take pleasure in simplicity, to make a good deal of magic with modest means."

Plan shows both levels, or wings, of the Connecticut house

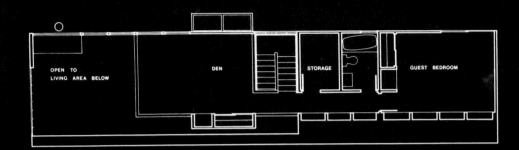

OPEN TO
LIVING AREA BELOW

DEN

STORAGE

GUEST BEDROOM

UPPER LEVEL   0   5   10

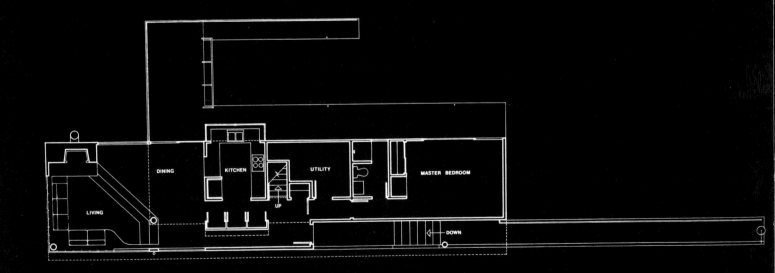

DINING

KITCHEN

UTILITY

MASTER BEDROOM

LIVING

UP

DOWN

LOWER LEVEL   0   5   10

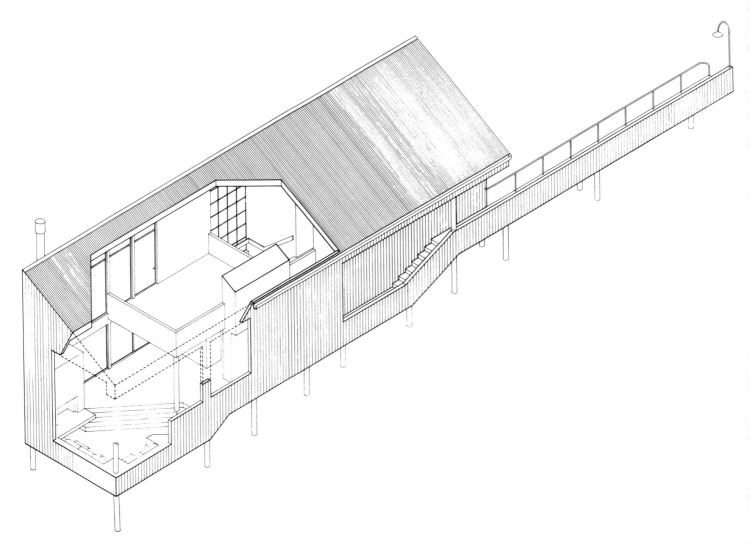

Cutaway drawing shows both circulation and volume in the house.

RIGHT **The house seems quite gently perched amid the trees.**

LAURINDA SPEAR AND BERNARDO FORT-BRESCIA

Harold and Suzanne Spear House

MIAMI SHORES, FLORIDA 1976–1979

I drive through the opening in the low white wall that surrounds the pink house, the pink palace of my childhood. The square concrete pavers of the driveway form a geometric grid with the green grass growing between them. The order and simplicity of the house and its meticulously organized landscape contrast the seemingly random placement of windows and the jagged stepping of the wall that mimics the stairs behind it. I sit on those stairs, with their long runs and low rises making the ascent to the front door easy, remembering how as a child I thought them so wide and challenging to climb. Now the two walls on either side of me, one dark red and the other medium pink, to emphasize the natural shadows, sandwich me between them. Strangely not one thing has changed . . . not even the distinctive smell of sea mixed with the odor of chlorine drifting from the lap pool on the other side of the wall.

Stepping up to the front door, I notice the generic doorknob of lusterless metal, and ring the simple rectangular doorbell, white against the light pink wall. The three o'clock sunlight plays with the five different shades of pink that force the perspective of the . . . walls. Palm, banana, and black olive trees are perfectly silhouetted against the house. Against a blue sky, the Pink House suggests the tropics; against the setting sun it blends with the pink sky; against the grayness of a thunderstorm its energy permeates me.—MARISA FORT, 1998

LEFT
The Pink House's more imposing façade looks out on Biscayne Bay

Harold and Suzanne Spear

Marisa Fort wrote this in her application to Barnard College, twenty years after her grand-parents' house was completed. She had not been born when it was designed, but she grew up knowing it intimately as her grandparents' house. This place, probably more than any other, formed her idea of what art is, what architecture is. The Pink House, as it came to be known, has its roots in a project Marisa's mother, Laurinda Spear, began as a graduate student at Columbia University. By the time Spear and her husband and partner, Bernardo Fort-Brescia, began working on the house in earnest, the design had been greatly modified. The Spear family had grown up just three blocks away, in a nondescript stucco house; the senior Spears, Harold and Suzanne, had long owned this prime bayfront site on which the Pink House was to be built—at the terminus of a street with a long and broad view across Biscayne Bay. Before their daughter was to become an architect, Harold and

Suzanne Spear had talked to other designers about the project, but had never made a decision to build. By the time the house was designed and built, all three children were grown and gone—sister Alison is also an architect, and "Hap" (Harold III) is a doctor.

Spear and Fort-Brescia—she was educated at Brown and Columbia; he at Princeton and Harvard—had recently married and co-founded their firm, Arqitectonica. Together, they set about the design of this house, starting with a look at building codes and long discussions with Harold and Suzanne Spear, a doctor and a writer, respectively. "My parents had a whole program," Spear says. "Mother had clippings, clippings, clippings—a myriad of ideas you couldn't possibly execute. My father asked for a lap pool, and that's all. If the truth be known, he probably wanted a Colonial house, not anything that anybody would notice. You have to understand that he was a doctor at a time when doctors viewed themselves very differently; he drove a Corvair to work, for example."

Whatever the senior Spears wanted, they got "pink." The house became an instant landmark—in many ways. It was the first widely published building for the partners-in-life architects of Arquitectonica. It also helped re-introduce color to a subtropical region that had fallen prey to blandness, though it was not alone in this. Simultaneously controversial and admired as a remarkable work of architecture, it is known intimately and internationally as the Pink House. A similarly sophisticated design might not have garnered much attention, but the shades of pink stucco made this house famous. The 1970s were still drab years in architectural colors. Laurinda Spear says that the choice of color was really a "personal bias." Even now, she says, "I think pink looks best in tropical settings. It contrasts with the sea and the sky. I thought it was sophisticated and aristocratic, like buildings in Nassau."

The house unfolds in layers. It is a long, narrow house (18 feet in width) running the breadth of the site, both for views and for breezes. The city side or west façade is scaled down to relate more to the other houses on the street. The bay side is scaled up to look monumental when viewed at a distance from a boat in the water or even from Miami Beach at the other shore. The description from Marisa Fort's essay resonates with both intimacy and affection:

> Upon passing through the threshold of the house, I step onto the smooth gray
> Cuban tiles of the patio, where to my right is the lap pool, and to my left is a gue-
> stroom. At the other end of the pool, overlooking it is the windows of what once
> was my great-grandmother's room. The ripples of water on the pool reflect on the
> white canvas canopy that cover a section of the patio, while the salty wind gently
> flaps it, creating the illusion of being on a sailboat. The first floor of the house, hot,
> humid, and lit with dramatic and bright shapes of sunlight is simple: all gray and
> white. Its double-height ceilings seem to mimic the sky making me feel miniscule,
> as if inside a monument of sorts. I cannot speak in the face of its overwhelming
> monochromatic abstract power. I concentrate on the architecture's focus: Biscayne

Bay and its beauty. The first view of it includes two of the islands that Christo surrounded in hot pink material. So many years before, I experienced this piece from the same place in front of the two-story wall of glass.

I feel the heat of the place pressing on me, reminding me of who I am, the city I am in. The house speaks to me as I sit on one of the two steep staircases mirroring each other at both ends of the long, arrow gallery. The gallery is flanked by sliding glass doors and by various rooms shooting off of it. The austerity of the house is unrelenting and imposing. Images of childhood rise within me like a flashflood. I recall running innocently from the enclosed patio, inside and upstairs to my grandparent's room. Each night before I fell asleep in the room where the two exterior walls are entirely glass, the house whispered to me "Miami," and each morning as the sun rose, it unveiled to me Miami.

Floor plan

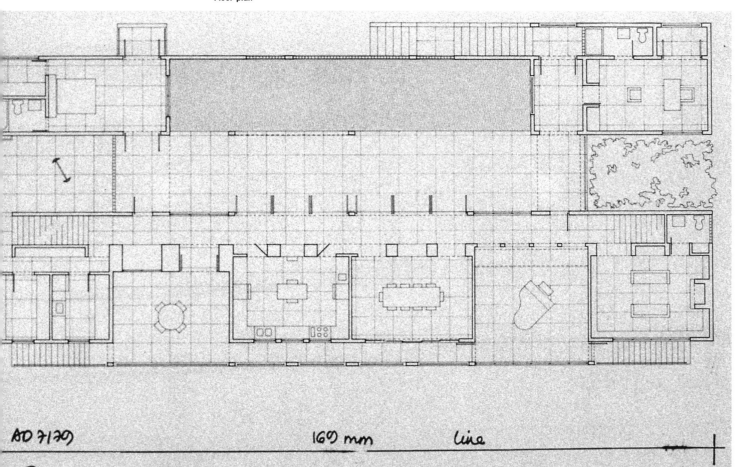

The front façade is graphic—and a study in layering. The house is painted in several different hues of pink.

RIGHT **Though one room opens onto another, rooms seem "framed" as if they were paintings.**

LAURINDA SPEAR AND BERNARDO FORT-BRESCIA

An early drawing by Laurinda Spear for her parents' house shows its villa-like proportions.

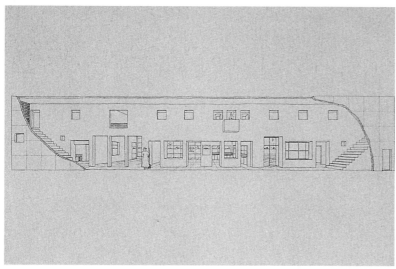

Elevation study for the Pink House

LAURINDA SPEAR AND BERNARDO FORT-BRESCIA

A long narrow lap pool framed by a stucco and glass block wall

The Izenour house sits close to the water's edge.

STEVEN IZENOUR
George and Hilda Izenour House
STONY CREEK, THIMBLE ISLAND, CONNECTICUT 1980

THE HOUSE THAT STEVEN IZENOUR DESIGNED FOR HIS PARENTS COMBINES THE HUMBLE WITH the glorious. It is self-effacing and boldly iconographic. Izenour is a principal in the firm of Venturi, Scott Brown and Associates, and co-authored the seminal work, *Learning from Las Vegas*, with Robert Venturi and Denise Scott Brown. He is not timid about taking simple architectural elements and making them bold.

This house, a neoclassical bungalow in inspiration, stands in the small island community of Stony Creek, east of New Haven and part of the Thimble Islands that dot the northern length of Long Island Sound. Stony Creek became a popular summer watering place over a hundred years ago, and, says Izenour, is a town filled with a "fine collection of shore homes dating from the mid-nineteenth century to the 1930s."

By the time George and Hilda Izenour asked their son to design a house for them, they were in their sixties and had spent more than thirty summers on one of the nearby Thimble Islands. The site of the new house had been used as a granite loading dock until the late 1920s, and then an oyster processing plant for four decades after that. Even after the oyster plant burned in the 1960s, the site still retained the visual legacy of its old buildings, a "picturesque tradition of weathered shingle sheds sitting on a massive granite pier," says Izenour.

This was to be a year-round home, a one-story house elevated against tidal action and flooding and braced against hurricane winds. The harsh winters on Long Island Sound dictated that the house have an enclosed garage as well.

George Izenour has had a prodigious career as a theater designer, and with his wife he has collected theatrical drawings and recordings of operas. Thus they needed a house fitted out with sophisticated sound and lighting systems for these collections, and with display space for a treasured set of rare Piranesi prints. Steven Izenour selected the rather simple typology of a bungalow, he says, "for its compact efficiency and sympathetic scale and profile with its neighbors." The house is clad in faded brown shingles. Still, it stands out. A

The house sits on a former loading dock for granite.

huge "ship's wheel" rose window—an allusion to the windows of Italian Renaissance cathedrals brought down to less vaunted use—presides over the north façade that faces front, to give the entrance a public scale. The window dominates the doorway and fills out almost the entire shingled gable. The entrance leads into the house and around the central fireplace into the vaulted living room. In turn, the living room opens out onto the porch and a view of Long Island Sound.

Outside, four flattened Doric columns, which echo the shape of the fireplace, support a sloping roof overhead while also framing the view—from the porch on the outside looking in and from the inside out. The side gable of the house rises above that, marked by a half-ship's wheel window, a gesture to Palladio. The half ship's-wheel window is again reiterated on the east and west facades. Izenour clad these facades in a diagonal shingle pattern (white against the faded natural shingles) to create a "Victorian decorative scale."

Izenour sought to fit the house into the context of its setting, yet to create a design that was novel and original. "This simple house is also interesting for what it is not," he says. "It does not use history by rote, nor does it use architectural style as superficial pastiche." Steve Izenour explains that the historic seashore bungalow form gives the house its scale and profile, and his design added "complex modern planned development, manipulation of scale in elevation, and a humorous dash of nautical symbolism."

A HOUSE ON LONG ISLAND SOUND · SECTION B-B

Cutaway view shows house, living room, and the setting.

RIGHT **The house needed to accommodate the Izenour's collection of Piranesi prints.**

Ross designed a showplace for both art and architecture.

MICHAEL FRANKLIN ROSS

John and Jean Ross House

OLD WESTBURY, LONG ISLAND, NEW YORK 1975–1981

Dear Michael,

I want to tell you that I really prefer double doors at the entrance because I think it has a more imposing look. If the same thing can be achieved with a one glass door, which I know Dad originally specified, then I guess I can be satisfied.

—JEAN ROSS to MICHAEL ROSS, May 1976

The house Michael Ross designed for his parents, John and Jean Ross, was an "empty nest" house, but that doesn't mean family was forgotten. The house was intended as a showplace for the achievements of two of the three Ross children—Michael the architect and Joanne the weaver. (The third, Marilyn, is a musician.) It also needed to be a painter's studio for Jean Ross and a retreat for John Ross, an insurance broker.

The Rosses found a heavily wooded two-acre site filled with fine and specimen trees, including hickory, black walnut, dogwood, cherry, and copper beeches in northern Long Island, once part of the vast holdings of a Long Island estate. The two acres offered a grade gentle enough to allow for construction but steep enough to look out to views down a hill and across a meadow.

As a young designer, Ross studied and taught in Japan under a Fulbright Fellowship. The time he spent there and the influence of Japanese architecture can be seen in the way the house sits on its site and connects back to nature. Ross began designing the house as an associate in the New York firm of Hardy Holzman Pfeiffer and completed it from Los Angeles where he had opened his own practice. Educated at Cornell and Columbia Universities, he is now managing director of the Los Angeles based firm SMP-SHG Incorporated.

The senior Rosses asked their son to design a house "with an open feeling." They asked for a three-bedroom house with the requisite living room, dining room, and kitchen along with the artist's studio and John Ross's den. They also requested he create physical separation between the two spare bedrooms and the master bedroom. "The house," says

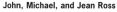
John, Michael, and Jean Ross

Ross, "is essentially a simple box that has been squeezed, bent, and eroded to respond to the site, to the circulation and to the specific requirements of the program. Its a box that settles into its sloping hillside to have a dialogue with nature." It uses curves, diagonals, and differing levels to undo the basic box, which is 50 by 50 feet. Importantly, the deviations from the rigid square shape of the box are insets in the house rather than protrusions from it, primarily, says Ross "to allow the trees to coexist with the house and the house to coexist with the trees. I was interested in achieving harmony with nature."

The house is clad in tongue-and-groove vertical cedar siding finished with a clear sealant. Windows are double-glazed and bronze-tinted. From the

entrance, the house's organization follows a skylighted "spine"—a pathway—that leads through the house and offers an interior view framed by stairs and a second-level skywalk. The interior is rotated 15 degrees within the box to maximize the views and the interior spaces are lofty enough to accommodate large woven wall hangings from Ross's sister, Joanne Schenendorf. Ross created the 15-degree shift to capture the views, and he says, "to add a dynamic to the house, a sense of surprise as you walk through it." The living room, dining room, and bedrooms also open out onto outdoor decks, reinforcing the easy indoor-outdoor connection.

The house began as a cube, then Ross cut into the basic geometry to get the final form.

The first floor is divided into three levels, to step down the site. An old and beautiful copper beech tree informed the shape of the house, as the architect "folded it in on itself" on the western corner. Inside, both eating areas—breakfast room and dining room—look out upon the terraced garden that has the copper beech as its centerpiece. The other important view is to the southeast, and the house is wrapped with a curved, two-story glass curtain wall looking in that direction.

The studio for Ross's mother presented its own set of requirements: Jean Ross asked that it be linked visually with the driveway, the living room, and the den. It needed north light, which was provided by the skylight, and a connection to the driveway to move stretched canvases in and large paintings out.

The Ross family has carefully preserved all the documentation of the process, in testimony to their close family ties. Both Jean and John Ross wrote a number of letters to their son in the course of the design process, including one on December 18, 1975, which concluded by saying "we are extremely excited as you know and are so lucky to share it with you and your expertise."

LEFT **Cutaway axonometric view of the Ross house: no rooms are actually square or rectangular.**

The site was once a large Long Island estate.

RIGHT **The living room connects interior spaces and the whole house with nature.**

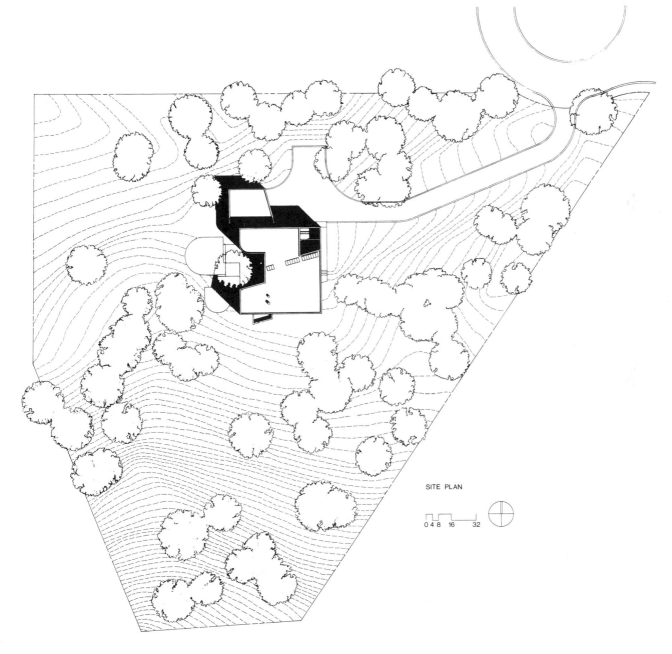

SITE PLAN

0 4 8   16   32

Site plan shows house's placement amid the trees.

The house is on a conventional street yet sited as if it were in the country.

PAUL WESTLAKE JR.

John and Carolyn Grima House

WARREN, OHIO 1983

FROM HIS EARLIEST CHILDHOOD, PAUL WESTLAKE JR., KNEW THAT ARCHITECTURE COULD TIE A family together, establishing bonds that were literally set in concrete. He had already seen this in his own family. Paul's uncle, Merle Westlake, a partner in the Cambridge, Massachusetts, firm of Hugh Stubbins and Associates, had designed a house in Cincinnati for his parents—Paul's grandparents.

It was in this way Paul Westlake was introduced to architecture. His uncle was a great admirer of Louis Kahn. Likewise, Westlake's parents took him to see numerous landmarks, including Frank Lloyd Wright's Taliesen West in Phoenix. "I never considered another profession," says Westlake, "In eighth grade I formally declared my intention in a career paper." Later, at the University of Pennsylvania, Westlake requested a dorm room that looked out on Kahn's Laboratory Facility. He went on to get two degrees (in business and architecture) at Penn then a master's in design from Harvard. His earliest positions were as an associate with the Cambridge Seven, Josep Luis Sert, and Louis Sauer.

In the early 1980s, after he had joined the Cleveland architectural firm now called VanDijk, Pace, Westlake & Partners, Paul Westlake received a commission that was entirely his own design—a house for his in-laws John and Carolyn Grima. It was his first opportunity "for uncensored, individual design work," he remembers. It also meant that every weekend he and his wife, Suzanne Grima Westlake, loaded their two small daughters in a car and traveled the 60-mile round trip from Cleveland to Warren, Ohio, to supervise the design and construction.

The house stands on a site that Westlake describes as "a conventional street flanked by close neighbors," yet it seems as if it were out in the country. A single magnificent oak tree dominates the site. The house is organized around a central axis. One goal was to offer both privacy and a connection to the outdoors. Thus there is a procession of outdoor and garden spaces, starting with a forecourt, a solarium that functions as a foyer and an interior garden, a courtyard, and a family room. The courtyard is a rarity in Northeastern Ohio, where the harsh winters are cold and wet. Yet in the pleasant-weather months of April through October, it is a much-welcomed inner sanctum. "The court, as a centerpiece, is the object of contemplation," said Westlake, "creating a sense of repose and place." The court's stone paving has gravel "reveals" to define the major axes in the house and meet at a focal point, which is made up of four copper squares.

The primary spaces of the house—living room, family room, kitchen, and dining room—encircle the courtyard. The master bedroom is on the first floor, set discretely back in a corner. A

BELOW
Carolyn and John Grima with granddaughter Emily Westlake

stairway from the foyer leads to a second-story study. A second stairway (one might call the back stairs) connects to two guest bedrooms, storage areas, and a deck that wraps around three sides of the courtyard; the deck is the only connection between the study and bedrooms.

The house is clad in cedar and has a regular, rhythmic progress of windows; some are large and some are small. Trellises and window trim are painted green, and these combined with the bright blooms of wisteria, azaleas, and other seasonal flowers are the one infusion of color against a natural palette, standing amid a simple landscape.

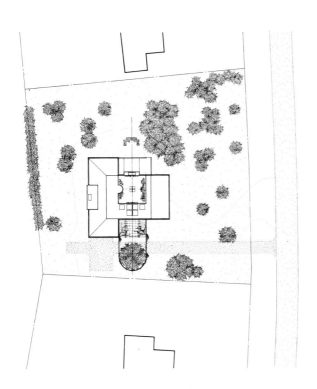

Site plan shows relationship of house to trees on lot and street.

Ground-floor plan shows circulation around the central courtyard.

The living room, with windows placed almost like paintings, looks out onto the courtyard.

Joan and David Crowell House

WASHINGTON, VERMONT 1973–1975

QUOGUE, LONG ISLAND, NEW YORK 1982–1984

MARK SIMON DESIGNED TWO HOUSES FOR HIS MOTHER, JOAN CROWELL, ONE IN THE MOUNTAINS and the other at the beach. In both cases, his mother asked him for a tower. Ultimately, she got her tower but it took her two tries.

The first time around, in the mountains, Simon designed an earth-sheltered house, which has a low profile. This house, set into the side of a hill in the mountains, explores both the local Vermont architectural vernacular and the energy benefits of earth sheltering. "Needless to say, my mother was a little nonplussed to find I had designed an underground house, but it just goes to show what a mother will do for a son."

In the early 1970s, Simon, then a recent Yale architecture graduate, and a group of friends had purchased a hillside site in northeastern Vermont as a commune farm; the land next door came up for sale, so they bought it. Then his mother, who had recently remarried, became interested in building a house on that site. "The thought of building my mother's house next to my hippie commune was devastating, but it just goes to show how desperate a young architect can be." The house was his second building design. Simon was then working for Charles Moore in New Haven, Connecticut, in a firm that evolved over the years into Centerbrook, where Simon is a partner. "I was pretty green at the time," Simon recalls.

The site was a significant one, a hill historically known for the long views it affords across to the Green Mountains, forty miles off in the distance. Simon decided to treat the

LEFT
The Quogue house, a composer's studio, was designed as a folly.

David Crowell, left, Joan Crowell, Mark Simon at the Crowell's wedding.

landmark landscape with as much reverence as he would hold for a historic building. Thus he designed the earth-sheltered house with an eye both to energy conservation and unobtrusiveness. The porch, the most visible aspect of the house, has a decorated gable, which was intended, Simon says, "to reassure nervous occupants that they are still in a house like

nearby farms and Victorian homesteads." The house needed to accommodate the two Crowells and allow for a limited number of visitors. It is a summerhouse (though usable in the winter), and it is just big enough for visiting offspring to use it one family at a time. The living room is the single major open space inside. There is a sleeping "inglenook" off the living room, a second bedroom, and a kitchen. Interior finishes are local wide-board white pine and exposed Douglas fir. Maple bobbins, manufactured locally for use in Southern mills, are set into walls "like Shaker pegs to hold vacation detritus," says Simon.

The house is concrete and buried on three sides, tucked under eighteen inches of sod aimed at both insulating it and shielding it from the sight-lines farther up the hill. The back walls are concrete, the structure exposed wood two-by-twelve-inch beams. There is flow-through ventilation. Though experimental at the time, the earth sheltering has proved to be successful; the house has never cooled below 31 degrees Fahrenheit, even when it was 30 degrees below Fahrenheit outside. Generally the concrete walls remain at 50 degrees through the cold of the Vermont winter. It is heated by two wood stoves and lit by gas lamps. The only electricity available is a back-up generator used solely for emergencies. A vapor barrier and air pocket between the interior siding and the concrete keep it cool and dry on muggy summer days, and it is ventilated by a system of skylights. "It's a wonderful place," says Simon. "You feel like you're truly in the wilderness."

The house in Vermont, though underground, emerged from the hillside with a porch that reflected local rural styles.

Years later, Joan Crowell asked her son to design another house, this one on the beach in Quogue, Long Island. Crowell and her husband had by then made Quogue their permanent residence. This was to be a composer's studio and private retreat. This site, like the earlier Vermont site, had magnificent views, but the outlook was over sand dunes to the Atlantic Ocean. "This time," said Joan Crowell to her son, "I want to make sure it has a tower." The desire for a tower had grown in its proportions over the ensuing decade; in Vermont it was a request, but in Quogue it was a mandate. Further, Crowell asked her son to design a walkway at the top of the tower. She wanted it not only for the views but also "to pace while creating."

Crowell wanted to use this house both as her composing studio and as a guesthouse and hideaway. She and her husband have their permanent residence in an adjacent house. The second structure, however, was to have all the basics—kitchen, dining room, bedroom, bathroom—and the main living space was to be Crowell's studio, a room capacious enough to accommodate a grand piano, a synthesizer, a computer. Says Simon, "We dubbed this house the Taj Mama."

In Quogue, an "old money" town on Long Island's south shore, the prevailing architectural motif is basically rather grand. Still, Simon remarks, "occasionally you'd see follies, most of them based on fake windmills." This house is a little more Anglo-Saxon. It is part windmill, part lighthouse—an octagonal tower domed with lead-coated copper rising above sloping hipped roofs. Both roofs and walls are clad in red cedar shingles, and the porch rails and roof overhangs are cedar latticework. Waterfront codes require lifting houses above the flood or tidal plane, so parking and storage are tucked underneath the house and hidden by more wood lattice, "a skirt," Simon terms it. The lattice "skirt" turns into a railing for the "long ambling stair" leading to the front door.

Large, double-hung windows facing south bring in sunlight, offering warmth. The living room/studio is further illuminated by three "piano key" skylights. The kitchen and dining areas are set off to one side, and the bedroom is up a broad stairway set under an arch. From the bedroom a second, steeper set of stairs leads to a tower room that is surrounded by the circular walkway. Inside, the soffit of the walkway becomes the frame of a bed. The tower's ceiling is the interior of the dome, which has a cupola on top to let in air and light.

The house recalls the fast-disappearing, quirky aspect of Long Island beach architecture; it is in many ways the realization of a romantic vision. Simon wanted this house to have that "rambling seaside spirit . . . but make no pretense of belonging to any but our time."

Section through the Quogue house

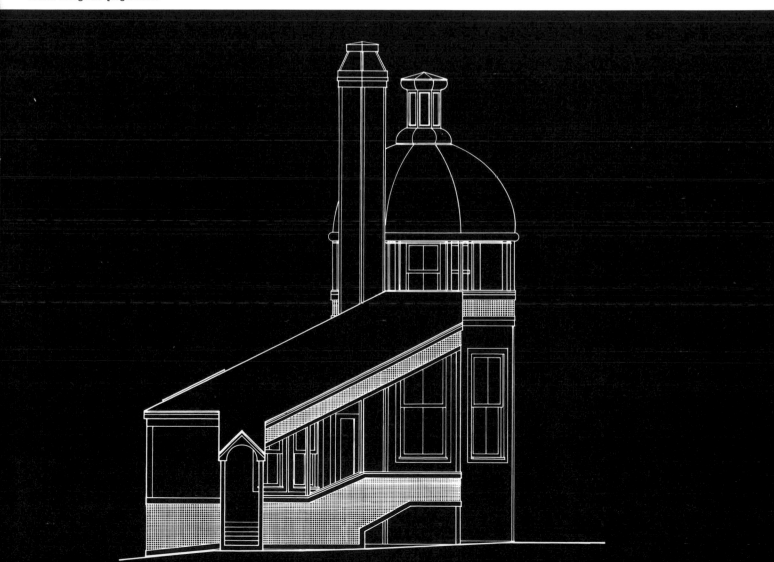

LEFT **The stairway curves gently as it climbs into the tower, which Joan Crowell asked her son to design.**

The main room of the house is actually a composer's studio with a piano as its centerpiece.

Bedroom and, below, floor plan

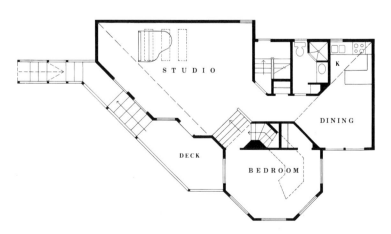

STUDIO

DINING

K

DECK

BEDROOM

RIGHT **The view back down to the house's covered terrace**

The Adams house replaced a deteriorated plantation house but kept both site and spirit of the old.

WALTER CHATHAM

William Howard and Janet Adams House

NEVIS, BRITISH WEST INDIES 1985

"BEFORE DISCOVERING NEVIS," WROTE WILLIAM HOWARD ADAMS IN AN ESSAY ABOUT THE house designed by his son-in-law Walter Chatham, "I thought the Caribbean was a little like Dr. Johnson's play that was worth seeing but not worth going to see. . . . I was not prepared for the sensual assault of the late-afternoon light, the shadows, the undulating foliage from all sides."

Chatham designed this house on Nevis in the British West Indies with an eye to local vernacular and island customs. He created it for his in-laws, William Howard and Janet Adams, whose daughter is Mary Adams, a furniture designer and the architect's wife. The house is located on the site of Montpelier Plantation, which had belonged to an early English Governor, Lord Herbert; Montpelier was where Herbert's daughter, the famous Fanny Nisbet, married Admiral Horatio Nelson. The elder Adamses had seen the site during a trip to the Caribbean in the early 1980s, which at the time was the site of a wooden house, a successor to the Herbert house. They bought it.

Their original idea was to renovate the house, but Chatham went to inspect his in-laws' purchase and discovered wood so riddled with termites that it had the strength of paper and shredded almost as easily. He developed a plan to rebuild based on the nineteenth-century stone foundation, working from the roots of the house at least. As time went on, however, Chatham discovered that even the foundation was not usable; it too had to be rebuilt. Still, all the other historic elements—wall outcroppings, gateposts, a privy house—were saved. Likewise Chatham was able to restore two eighteenth-century cisterns on the site, returning them to their original pyramidal form and preserving their powerful presence on the landscape.

Walter Chatham, second from left, with William Howard and Janet Adams, right, during construction.

The senior Adamses had one stipulation: that the craftsmanship all be local. The island of Nevis is comparatively inaccessible, so that imported building materials are not commonplace; thus millwork, including shutters and louvers, was all done on site. Floors are paved with local field stones. One piece of the house is actually indigenous to the island, though not the site. While touring the island one day, the Adames found a small house that had fallen into disuse. "My father-in-law, ever the intrepid bargainer, saw the house, bought it, and had it moved," says Chatham. Thus one bedroom is a Nevis original. The plan for the house remained much as it had been in its "found" condition, though nothing of the original was to remain. There were changes of course, notably interior corridors became exterior passageways, as well as an open-air dining pavilion and a living room that face the sea.

In the house, the bedrooms are set back, to accord somewhat more privacy. In the fashion of Caribbean architecture, there are no

Site plan shows house on its historic seaside site.

actual windows, simply shuttered openings; the two principal rooms are essentially open-air porches. In deference to local building traditions, the house has a base made from cast concrete block and a second story of wood.

For Chatham, the idea of discovery underlies the design. The house seems almost opaque upon arrival and opens up as one approaches it and walks into it, to a view of the sea beyond. The forms of the house are simple but powerful, steep-roofed pavilions with rhythmically spaced colonnades, like an assemblage of small classical temple buildings on a dramatic site above the sea.

Floor plans for first, right, and second stories.

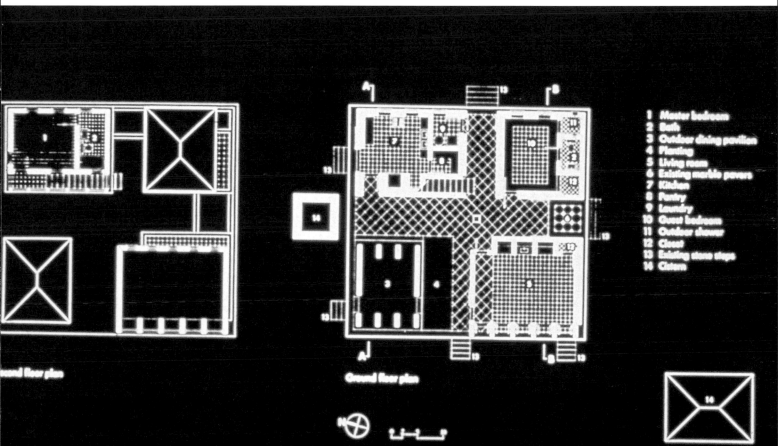

1 Master bedroom
2 Bath
3 Outdoor dining pavilion
4 Planting
5 Living room
6 Existing marble pavers
7 Kitchen
8 Pantry
9 Laundry
10 Guest bedroom
11 Outdoor shower
12 Closet
13 Existing stone steps
14 Cistern

Second floor plan

Ground floor plan

An upstairs bedroom, furnished simply, and sitting under the eaves

Drawing for Adams house shows siting and sequencing.

The dining room is a pergola-like room, typical of Caribbean living.

The walkway between the two pavilions is paved in local stone.

The Shoar house design relies on symmetry and simplicity.

SUZANNE MARTINSON

Mel and Avanell Shoar House

PUNTA GORDA, FLORIDA 1985

SUZANNE MARTINSON OPENED HER OWN ARCHITECTURAL PRACTICE WITH ONE COMMISSION in hand: a house for her mother and stepfather, Avanell and Mel Shoar, to be built on a waterfront site on Florida's western Gulf Coast. Some years before, the Shoars had bought the land that looks out on an estuary leading to Charlotte Harbor, awaiting the time when they could build there.

This is a waterside house for boatbuilders. The Shoars build their own sailboats, and as such they look for efficiency and economy in the way space is used. They also have implicit aesthetic expectations about how space is treated. Beyond these more intangible character-istics—which Suzanne Martinson knew instinctively, even if her mother and stepfather did not state them directly—the wooden-boatbuilders made only one specific request of their architect: the house was to have no wood, just concrete and metal. Other design conditions were more practical. The Shoars wanted a cistern to collect the rain; Punta Gorda's climate is arid and irrigation water occasionally falls into short supply. Town zoning mandated that the house had to be lifted above the ground to bring it above the flood plain. There were aesthetic reasons to do so, as well: a higher house would capture the breezes, keeping it cool and airy, and would offer longer views across the densely vegetated mangroves.

The house has a strong presence, but it is also uncomplicated. Martinson has long been interested in what she calls "elegant simple solutions" to architectural problems. "And my mother, being Scandinavian, has never liked ornate things. She likes everything to be very sparse," Martinson says.

Suzanne Martinson is a tenacious modernist but one who does not deny the past. To give the design a certain form she studied Italian farmhouses, Southern "dog trot" houses, and the Mediterranean villas that prevailed in Florida in the 1920s. Hence the house's

Avanell Shoar, Suzanne Martinson, and Mel Shoar hang out the construction sign for their new house.

shape and proportions, built in concrete block and stucco. It has a sloping tile roof and a simple rectilinear form. "I wanted the envelope of the building to give it scale and spatial pleasure," said Martinson. "I wanted it to look like a house."

It is a sturdy house, as well, constructed of concrete blocks, white stucco, and black metal. The front is solid, for greater privacy; it opens out to the back, to the views and the breezes. For the same reasons, the primary living quarters are on its second floor, with a guest bedroom and a workshop below. The house is symmetrical and easy to read.

It is also practical for the climate. The Shoars, as sailors and Floridians, were energy conscious. Thus came the spanning roof to create "incredible shade with its big overhangs" of five feet. The house is heated by the sun and cross-ventilated; it faces south, which means that it catches the prevailing breezes during the hottest months—April through October—and yet stays warmer in the winter when the wind shifts to the north. The Shoars rarely use air-conditioning.

The positioning of the house was quite deliberate. The workshop, Mel Shoar's hide-away, is in complete shade while offering a clear view of the water. This boatbuilder never feels too distant from the sea. "Nice natural things happen," says Martinson as she describes the house's natural orientation, "Mother can lie in bed and see the moon rise, for example."

Though the exterior form is traditional, interior spaces are modernist. Martinson sought to create a certain "boat aesthetic," using nautical elements such as stainless steel cable for railings. Her refined eye for interior details and spaces stems from her original training as an interior designer. Martinson then completed an undergraduate architectural degree at the University of Miami, and had just completed graduate school at Columbia University when she designed the Shoar house. She worked for Mark Hampton in Miami and Kohn Pederson Fox in New York City, before opening her own office in Miami, where she had grown up and still lives.

In Miami, where the climate is subtropical and wet much of the year, the Shoars had cultivated a luxuriant tropical garden. Punta Gorda, however, is comparatively dry and not conducive to the same kind of gardening and Martinson brought in plants and trees prior to construction, using landscape to help frame the house and introduced planters on top of cistern. There she planted bougainvillea, a symbolic plant of the tropics and one that actually grows better in adverse climatic conditions. It has flourished and provides the primary color for a house that otherwise has a Scandinavian sensibility and the considered control of boat design.

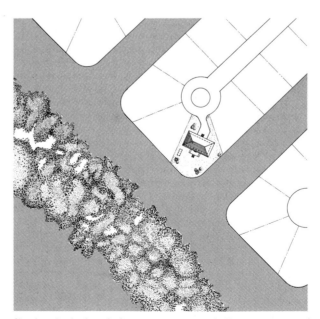

Site plan, showing house's placement on a waterway looking out at a mangrove.

RIGHT **Axonometric cutaway view of second floor.**

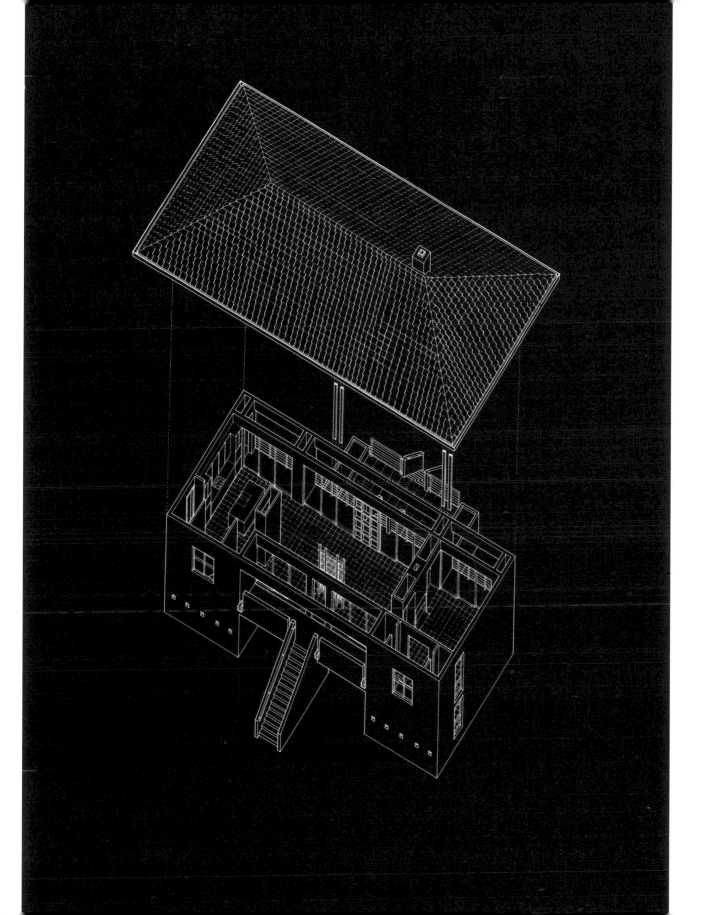

Second-floor living room has a waterview and opens to the prevailing breezes.

BELOW **Second floor plan.**

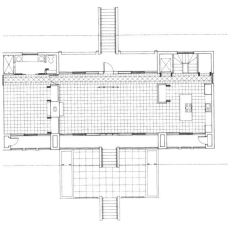

RIGHT **The house allows for indoor and outdoor living.**

The open plan affords free flowing coastal breezes.

SUZANNE MARTINSON

Steep overhangs and porches shade house from sun while allowing for natural cooling.

Len and Jan Lesniak House

BAY HEAD, NEW JERSEY 1989

DAVID LESNIAK WAS FINISHING HIS GRADUATE WORK AT THE UNIVERSITY OF PENNSYLVANIA when his parents called to say they had bought a vacant house lot in the shore town of Bay Head, New Jersey. They wanted him to design the house, a weekend retreat.

Bay Head is a quaint town, streets lined with nineteenth-century clapboard and shingle cottages. Lesniak began looking around for inspiration. Indeed, "much was generated by what was in town. It was very much a little shingle community." He even went to the town's archives for local historical sources. Lesniak also turned to the work of Robert A. M. Stern, who had recently published *The Architecture of the American Summer,* which featured several Bay Head houses. For further references, he looked at the work of Robert Venturi, "because it was so spirited," Lesniak explains. "I didn't want to do a period piece."

The lot his parents had bought was long and narrow; it had been carved out of two sideyards of older, existing houses. Lesniak decided, quite literally, to slip the house in, and set it back as if it had been built as a guest cottage—not to compete with the other houses. This is exactly what he wanted, in order to gain more privacy for the back yard and a size-able front yard for his mother's profuse English-style gardens.

Lesniak had worked in New York City for four years after completing his under-graduate architecture degree at Washington University—first at Beyer Blinder Belle and then Gensler & Associates. Then he went to graduate school. Even with his work experience and six years of architecture school, he had never run a job start-to-finish. "It was an incredible opportunity," he says, "but by the same token, a lot of it was by the seat of my pants."

From the front, the house appears a modest cottage, older even, but perhaps one with new windows. It has a broad

LEFT
The "hallway" of the house is a two-story space that doubles as dining room and central circulation.

Len and Jan Lesniak on the front porch of their Bay Head house

front porch and a centered gable. On the side elevation, the house takes on the lines and proportions of a shingle-style house, albeit a stripped down one. Two wide, symmetrical gables with kick-slopes at the end dominate this face. A central cupola rises up to join the connecting space that spans the gables.

That connecting space is the house's single grand, and somewhat modern, gesture. It is a two-story hallway that doubles as a formal dining room—Len and Jan Lesniak's primary requirement. From the hallway, a stairway rises up and divides, leading into each of the gabled second-story areas. The dining room's three large windows face east, even though the house is not on the waterfront, a symbolic gesture as if the house actually did open onto the sea. "When you're in the dining room, all you see is the sky," he says.

The interior details came largely from Len and Jan Lesniak's observations about the town's historic architecture. They had owned a condominium apartment nearby and had spent a good deal of time taking in the historic surroundings, to apply it in their new house. Thus David Lesniak used building techniques and interior finishes of older houses in the area to this new one. One example is the ceiling beams on the first floor, which are the joists from the floor above. "It's a little noisy," he says, " but that's how it's locally done."

The doors are all mismatched, on purpose. Lesniak consciously designed the house to seem as if it had grown, been added to, and changed over time. "It wasn't intended to be a finished sort of house," he explains. During construction, Jan Lesniak found seven stained-glass windows and bought them, saying to her son, "I love these. Can we use them?" Scattered throughout the house are the seven stained-glass windows. The furniture, too, is an aggregation. Some pieces came from the Lesniak's suburban Wayne, New Jersey, house, the former family home. Others are finds from antique shops or thrift stores, "as the spirit moved us." The couch in the living room belonged to Jan Lesniak's mother.

In 1997 Len and Jan Lesniak began living in Bay Head year-round. Their son, meanwhile, had bought a house in town. It's not new. Indeed it is a century-old balloon-framed cottage, "a true Bay Header," he says. He respects the differences between the old and his new. But its actually commonplace, and rather nice, for David Lesniak to be asked when he designed the renovations and additions to his parents' house.

LEFT **Columns frame the passage from one room to another.**

The long side of the house highlights the shingle-style inspiration.

RIGHT **Plan elevation of the house shows the hallway/dining room combination.**

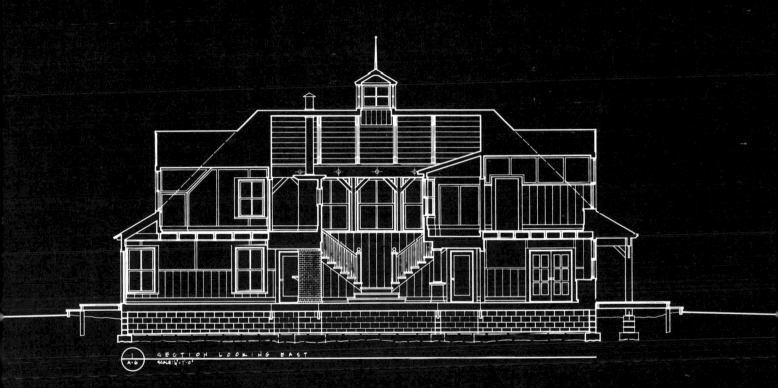

SECTION LOOKING EAST
SCALE: ¼" = 1'-0"

RIGHT The house was built using many traditional construction techniques.

BELOW Front elevation of house shows porch, gable, and cupola.

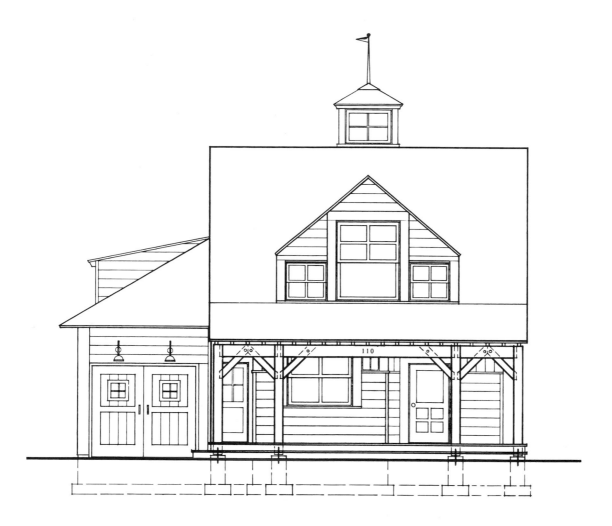

ROBERT KAHN

Lawrence and Jane Kahn House

ST. LOUIS, MISSOURI 1988–1990

ROBERT KAHN HAD GROWN UP IN A MODERN HOUSE IN ST. LOUIS, ONE DESIGNED BY WILLIAM Bernoudi, a well-known Midwestern architect and a disciple of Frank Lloyd Wright. That house sat on three suburban acres, and was much beloved by the whole family. Still, many years later, Lawrence and Jane Kahn decided to move to a smaller house.

They found a quarter-acre lot nestled amid older houses in a established suburban neighborhood of St. Louis. By then, Robert Kahn—a graduate of Yale School of Architecture and a Rome Prize winner—had established his own practice in New York after an apprenticeship with British architect James Stirling. Though it might seem that the Kahns had waited until their son had some experience under his belt, he says, "they didn't do it on purpose, but they were lucky that I'd done a few houses on my own already." Still the move was fraught with emotion: "It was hard moving from the house we'd all grown up in. And of course, there was a lot of pressure on me because I was the one who was designing it."

Lawrence and Jane Kahn (he is a doctor, and she is a social worker) were knowledge-able clients. Art collectors, they were also quite astute about architecture. And of course, they had already commissioned the design of one house. Of the two, Lawrence Kahn was more reluctant to move, "even though," says his son, "he was going to design the new house." As an avid gardener who relished the privacy afforded by a large suburban lot, he essentially set the script. The house had to seem "luxurious in terms of its gardens," he told Robert, and yet offer a great deal of privacy.

In the new house's neighborhood, the residences are essentially boxes set back 25 feet from the street, with ceremonial front yards and tiny back yards consumed by driveways and parking and enclosed by fences. House and yard have little relationship to one another, just a co-existence.

"I immediately knew I wanted to build the house around a garden, and treat the garden as if it were another room in the house, and not in a clichéd way," says Kahn.

He stretched the house's footprint to the maximum extent allowed by the zoning to come up with a layout "that is best described as a courtyard or a Roman house plan. In Rome, in the first suburbs, the houses were cheek to jowl but they had privacy because they opened up onto a garden."

Thus came a house with distinct elements—guest suite, study, living/dining room, kitchen, master bedroom—an idea that ultimately led Kahn to develop a "kit of parts," essentially a sophisticated building block system to help clients envision the house they are building. One wing of the house includes a "long bar piece" of two stories hugging one edge of the site; it contains guest bedrooms, bathrooms, and a study. Next to that is the living room, with its vaulted ceiling, a grand room with its own distinctive shape, height, and volume; it is big enough to accommodate a dining table at one end, thereby eliminating the need for a separate dining room. A row of glass doors open out onto the courtyard garden to create a significant and striking space.

"People are always taken aback when they see this space, but equally impressive, or shocking even, is that you are suddenly looking through the living room at this incredibly lush garden, almost as if you had walked into a secret back yard," says Kahn. The living room connects to the kitchen and master bedroom, which, like the living room, has a "big sloping ceiling," Kahn says. The bedroom is exposed to sculptured nature, in one direction looking out to the planted courtyard and in the other to a little water garden.

The housing of cars—a ubiquitous problem in the suburbs—challenged Kahn to design a pergola that acts both as a garden element and a car park. A botanical view is always in sight. The garden was planted so that it would have form and beauty year round: two Japanese maples offer shade in the summer and become exquisite sculptural elements in the winter.

The wood-clad house is painted gray with white trim; the porch is blue. Kahn thinks of the design as vernacular modern. He sought a certain timelessness, so he gave the house numerous traditional elements and a definite respectful quality. "I think most good ideas have existed before. I'm not very interested in architecture in terms of fashion, in terms of what's trendy. However, I do think that the architecture of a building should say something about the time in which it was done."

Indeed, Kahn says, "this is not a center-hall Colonial." The room layout and detailing are modern. The house is wooden but not clapboard. The porch—the entrance to hearth and home—is made of steel instead of wood. Windows are stylized and clearly new, rather than the typical double hung variety; they are set into pronounced frames, which become the house's primary ornamental detailing. Along the way, as Kahn designed, a real rigor entered the design. "If I couldn't explain it, we eliminated it," he says.

Of course, as in any architect's design, there is much here that is drawn from instinct: Kahn knew he was shouldering a big burden when he designed the replacement for what was not simply the time-honored family house but a local (and personal) icon of modernism. To do so meant finding the right balance between rigor and sentiment, to find the threads that would tie the family together, that would make the new place one that seemed to belong the family.

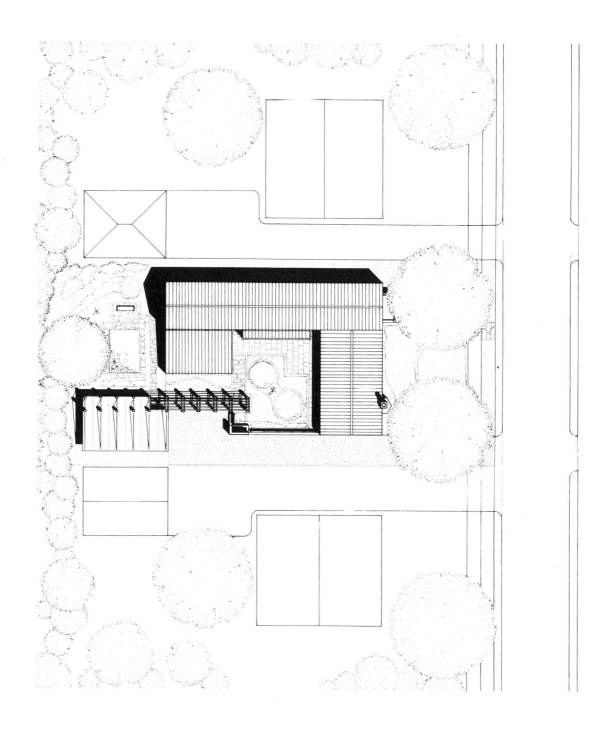

Site plan of house shows the placement of the two gardens.

The long and narrow kitchen looks out on the garden.

RIGHT **The vaulted dining room ceiling**

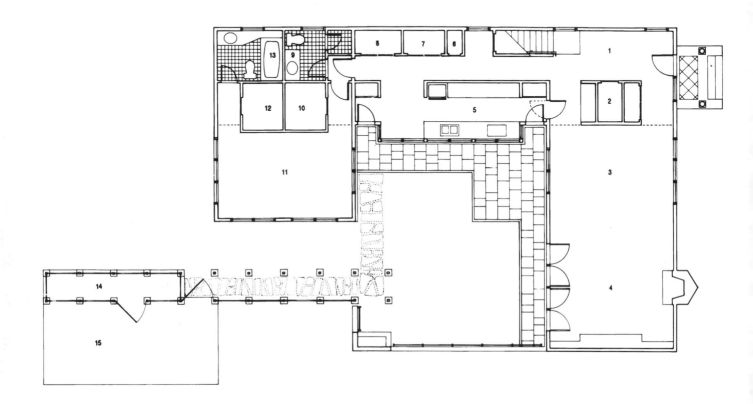

1. FOYER
2. CLOSET
3. DINING ROOM
4. LIVING ROOM
5. KITCHEN
6. MECHANICAL ROOM
7. LAUNDRY
8. CLOSET
9. BATHROOM
10. CLOSET
11. MASTER BEDROOM
12. CLOSET
13. MASTER BATHROOM
14. STORAGE
15. CARPORT

Entry level plan shows relationship of indoor and outdoor spaces.

The Caldwell beach house has two very different faces, this one for the street side.

NATALYE APPEL

Tom and Carolyn Caldwell House

GALVESTON ISLAND, TEXAS 1990

THE BEACH HOUSE NATALYE APPEL DESIGNED FOR HER PARENTS IS A HOUSE WITH TWO FRONT-yards. It sits between a busy beach road and a far more tranquil beach, and the house makes peace between the two. It is a house with the casual, eccentric feel of a beach shack and the rigor of a thoroughly disciplined work of architecture.

Appel's parents, Tom and Carolyn Caldwell, had owned an unremarkable cottage on the bayfront of Galveston Island and had longed to go to the gulf side; it was not until Hurricane Alicia took its toll in 1983 that circumstances gave them the opportunity. The Caldwells were in no real hurry and had no special constraints "except a budget, which was tiny—a low per square foot budget but also low square footage," says their daughter-architect.

Appel, who now heads a Houston architectural firm bearing her own name, was then a young Rice University architecture graduate on her way to the University of Pennsylvania graduate school. With time on her side, she began working on studies for the house, wandering through Galveston's various neighborhoods, looking at houses. As she took in the island's charming vernacular architecture, she also confronted a problem affecting many of the newer houses there. They were sandwiched between road and beach, their best façade turned away from the public street. "Generally, everything faces the water, and all the bad stuff hangs out on the road," says Appel.

Her notion for this house was to create two distinct countenances for two very different perspectives—one for the town and one for the beach. "I called it the highway house, or the billboard house," she says. On the highway side, the house is basically closed off, though it has a "face." There is a blue tower set against a flat wall clad in cedar shakes. Both tower and shingled wall are punctuated with small rectangular windows.

The tower actually encases a stairway. Like most contemporary beach houses, this one is lifted off the ground and set on pilings. Appel looked at it as an opportunity to make the house more town-friendly, tying it back to the colonnaded structures in European cities. The back wall serves as a kind of screen; it houses service functions (primarily bathrooms) while it largely shields the house from the road and presents an abstract, artistic face to the outside world.

Carolyn, left, and Tom, front right, celebrating a birthday with three grandchildren

From the beach, however, the house looks exactly like what it is: a beach shack gone sophisticated. The body of the house is actually two connected pavilions—one houses the living room and master bedroom, and the other contains the kitchen and two additional bedrooms. One pavilion has a single slope to it, half a shed one might say; the other is pyramid-topped. Natural light streams in between the two pavilions, and even more essential, plenty of sea-air breezes. The division has climatic benefits, and very important psychological ones as well. When several generations of family members gather in a 1,700-square-foot beach house, says Appel, "You have the feeling of being in your own little beach shack."

The kitchen with its view of the surf made the most of limited space.

The house's contractor built the house to the finished shell, then the Caldwells did the rest themselves. "It gave us the opportunity to really think about it and be creative with materials," Appel says.

Tom Caldwell bought unpainted cabinets and finished them himself. Carolyn Caldwell laid the kitchen and bathroom tiles. And for her part, Appel searched for inexpensive and ingenious materials for such elements as the tub surround (a translucent green corrugated fiberglass from a boating supply store) and the stair railings (which are made of plumbing pipes). The floors are made of durable, if unpretentious, two-by-six sub-flooring, finished as if they were a top layer

Seaside imagery abounds. The railing's wood supports are shaped like boat rudders. Wall finishes include beaded board and shiplap. And, as in a sailboat, every space has a use: windowsills are wide to become window seats, storage is tucked away under the benches, and in such rooms as the kitchen, all the vertical space is employed with stowing or showing cookware and foodstuffs. "We wanted everything to be rough-and-tumble but warm," says Natalye Appel.

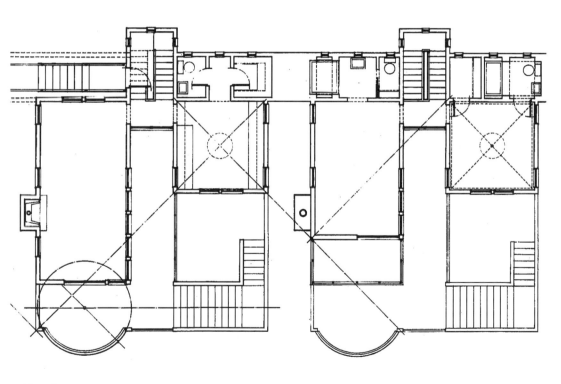

Floor plan

TOM AND CAROLYN CALDWELL HOUSE

Appel made the most of the "beach shack" vernacular found in Galveston Island.

LEFT **At grade, the house leads from street to beach.**

The kitchen with its view of the surf made the most of limited space.

RIGHT **The side view shows how the beach house mitigates two differing conditions, busy roadway and idyllic sand dunes.**

Charles and Lisa Menefee House

HURRICANE GAP, NORTH CAROLINA 1990–1992

CHARLES MENEFEE GREW UP ON WADMELAW ISLAND JUST SOUTH OF CHARLESTON, SOUTH Carolina, in a family that kept to such traditions as gathering around the dining table and lingering there. Perhaps less traditionally, the Menefee family lived in a modern house designed for them by Miami architect Alfred Browning Parker. Lisa Menefee had seen one of Parker's houses in an issue of *House Beautiful* magazine, and asked Parker to adapt a house he had designed for the near-tropics of southern Florida to the sticky, humid conditions of the coastal Carolinas.

Their son, Charles, was six years old when that house was designed, and, he says, "that was a grand and exciting thing to have happened. It was designed for a particular landscape, a flat river savanna that is hit by hurricanes but is also in a mild earthquake zone and subject to two kinds of termites, as well as salt air. And we had no air-conditioning."

Menefee's early exposure to the design process was all-informing. Some three decades later, he found himself creating for his parents their second architect-designed house, this one a mountain getaway. While the house of his childhood was on flat coastal land, this one was to be a mountain house at an elevation of some 3,000 feet in a "vertical environment." The site is a hardwood forest, in an area where one has to ascend to get a view. "In South Carolina, you can see the sky for distances; here, you have to climb to see the sky," Menefee explains.

LEFT
The house is nestled into its mountainside site, climbing as the terrain rises.

Like the landscape, the house is vertical. It is constructed of unfinished concrete blocks and basically climbs the mountain. The roof is slightly vaulted and set above the house as if it were floating. The effect, says Menefee, "is of being way up in the air, like a treehouse. The wall ends, and the roof floats above the wall so you can see the ridgeline across the valley."

In response to practical considerations, the house is designed to require almost no maintenance. It has to withstand termites, brush fires, high winds, snow, driving ice rain, lightning strikes—and bears. And although the last danger might seem unusual in the less-rugged-than-the-Rockies mountain environment of North Carolina, Menefee counters, "A year ago my parents sent me a photo where there were bear paws on the glass."

Another consideration was that Charles and Lisa Menefee wanted to get to know a landscape that was very new to them. "The house became a lens through which to look at the landscape," their son says. "And the change is not at all subtle in the mountains, which

Upstairs the rooms have a treehouse-like feel.

was something they really wanted to enjoy. My mother can get up close and look at a cater-pillar crawling by, and my father can sit back in a chair and enjoy the changing colors of the distant landscape."

The windows are ample enough to see a wide panorama. Charles Menefee sought to impart the sense that the whole wall disappears. In some seasons—summer and to a lesser extent spring and fall—the whole house opens up. Another aspect of the house goes back to Menefee family traditions: Charles Menefee cannot remember a time when the whole family did not sit down together for dinner. In the old Wadmelaw Island house, that meant gathering around an eight-foot cypress table outside; here, in the smaller mountain house, there is no porch, nor is the climate welcoming to eating outdoors most of the year. The imperative remained. Thus came a smaller table, and though it sits inside the house, the connection to the outdoors is still there. "It still supports the same [large] family gathering around a table even if its only four feet in diameter," says Menefee, "but it is still the same family with the same culture and the same habits."

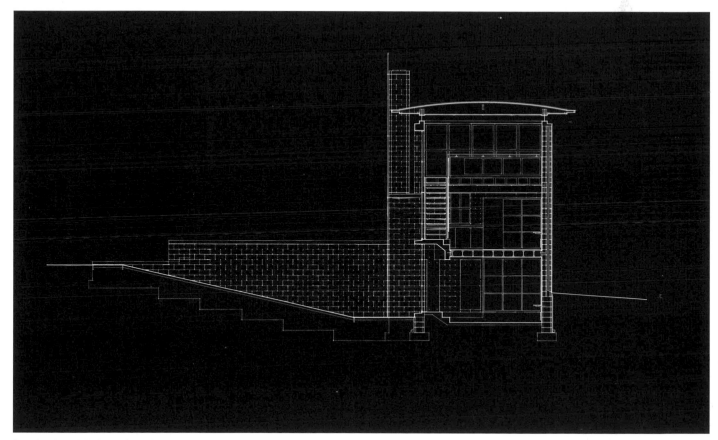

A section through the house shows the three-story circulation.

Bedrooms look over the forested site

A staircase functions almost like a ladder between floors.

The mountain getaway reflects its "vertical" environment.

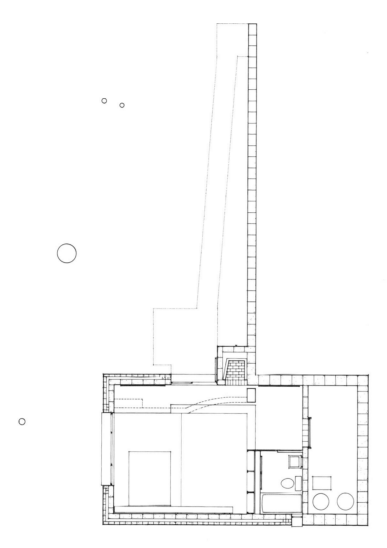

The house opens up to and bears down on the mountain site.

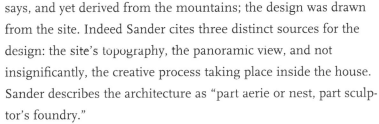

WHITNEY SANDER
John and Gretchen von Storch Swift House

BRECKENRIDGE, COLORADO 1992–1994

WHITNEY SANDER'S NEWLY REMARRIED MOTHER CALLED HIM ONE DAY WITH AN URGENT request, asking him to go to Breckenridge, Colorado, and look at a piece of property. His mother and stepfather, Gretchen von Storch Swift and John Swift, thought they'd found just the right site for a house. They planned to move to Colorado for retirement.

The land they found was four acres on a hill 10,000 feet above sea level. "The property was gorgeous," Sander remembers. It was a high-up hillside with vast views out to the mountain ranges beyond. The Swifts, however, didn't want a shake-clad ski chalet; they wanted a house for artists that itself was a work of art. They wanted it to be dramatic and modern—a house for sculptors that conveyed "the meaning of [the artist's] process and product."

LEFT
The long view looks out to Colorado's Ten Mile Range.

BELOW
The design—a metaphor of body, skin, and spine

Sander designed a sleek contemporary house and urged the community design board to approve it. The Breckenridge locals scoffed. "It was definitely not in mountain style," he says, and yet derived from the mountains; the design was drawn from the site. Indeed Sander cites three distinct sources for the design: the site's topography, the panoramic view, and not insignificantly, the creative process taking place inside the house. Sander describes the architecture as "part aerie or nest, part sculptor's foundry."

He worked with the metaphorical idea of the body, of skin and spine, as he designed the house. Indeed, Gretchen Swift had seen a house her son had designed in Hillsborough, California. She had been particularly taken by its curving front wall and thus asked for something based on the same idea. "The design idea was to place the house so that it looked out across a small valley at the Ten Mile Range—ten mountain peaks, two of which are the Breckenridge ski area. I set up the house with a long view, and the curve then became the front face," Sander says. "Its a design only a mother could love."

From its lofty perch, it is like a treehouse that has a certain amount of abstraction. The roof curves towards the view as the 35-foot front wall curves along the view. "As you approach it, you turn onto the driveway and you see the incredible view," Sander says.

The house is organized along a circulation corridor. One enters on the uphill side, the back of the house, and walks along a central spine housing gallery space that showcases the sculptor's pottery and other artwork. Beyond is the "great room," the main room of the house, with windows all along it, opens out through the lodgepole pines to the mountains beyond. It is all very dramatic: the corridor is low and leads into the airy "great room" with its curved wall of windows and a 16-foot ceiling. At the far end is a study, which looks out into the trees instead of across to the mountains. An outside deck that wraps the curved wall unites the house and environment.

The bedrooms line up behind the great room, "sliding along the view." Downstairs are guestrooms and a bathroom. Far below, "burrowed into the steep slope," is the sculptor's studio, a brilliantly lighted space of ten-foot windows.

The house is clad in stucco and stone, with wood windows and a tar-and-gravel roof. The stone façade faces the uphill side. The 35-foot windowed wall faces the view, a dramatic and unexpected sweep of a façade. Though the windows that line it are actually standard, three-foot window increments, smaller clerestory windows above capture the eastern morning sun. "I didn't want the complexity of the window to obscure the curve," says Sander. The wooden window frames actually shape the view in a way a vast expanse of glass could not.

His mother and stepfather had been trained early on as artists, though they turned elsewhere (into education) for their work until retirement, when both—primarily John Swift—returned to their original callings. "Both retained an aesthetic sensibility," Sander explains, which made the house a collaborative venture more than typically found between the architect-client. Sander, who holds undergraduate and graduate degrees from Yale University, looks at the design of this house as a watershed—perhaps less for design than for carving new meanings in their relationships. "We were all transformed by the interactions as our roles shifted and alternated between profession, concerned son, client, mother, new family member," he says. "It brought us closer . . . and provided us with the opportunity to set and explore each other's roles and limits. To a large extent, our present relationship is still charged with the experience of creating that house."

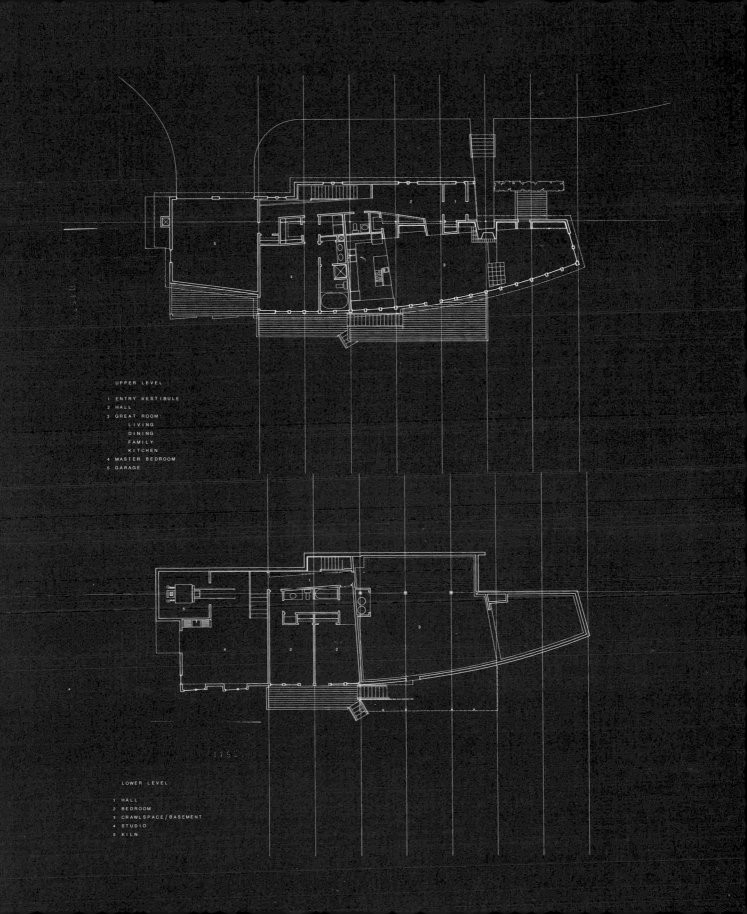

UPPER LEVEL

1 ENTRY VESTIBULE
2 HALL
3 GREAT ROOM:
       LIVING
       DINING
       FAMILY
       KITCHEN
4 MASTER BEDROOM
5 GARAGE

LOWER LEVEL

1 HALL
2 BEDROOM
3 CRAWLSPACE/BASEMENT
4 STUDIO
5 KILN

A stained glass panel designed as an abstraction of the plan of the house

LEFT The house's façade curves through the tall pines.

A spare living room focuses out to the family's view of nature.

RIGHT The house serves as a sculptor's gallery, a showcase for Von Storch's ceramics and sculpture.

The house draws on the imagery of the local rural architecture.

ROBERT LUCHETTI

Lawrence and Petra Luchetti House

MIDDLETON, COYOTE VALLEY, CALIFORNIA 1994

ROBERT LUCHETTI'S PARENTS HAD OWNED AN OLD CATTLE RANCH IN COYOTE VALLEY AN HOUR north of Napa, California, since 1970. When they bought it, there was a wooden Victorian ranch house on the land, but later it burned to the ground. For years, when they went to visit, family members had stayed in the old caretaker's cabin and several trailers plunked down on the site.

Over the years, the family had turned it into a working ranch with four bulls used as sires and hay harvested and sold. It was a sideline—a ranch run by others—while the members of the Luchetti family plied their professions elsewhere. Still, when they gathered, it was at the cabin and the trailers. "We'd been talking of building a house there for years," says Robert Luchetti. One day, Lawrence Luchetti called each of his seven children with a challenge: he could build a house to be used for big family gatherings, long weekends, and vacations, but the house would become the family's primary inheritance. Unanimously, the family voted for a house.

Thus came a highly sophisticated barn, a rural house with an edge to it. Inside and out, the Luchetti house draws on ranch-inspired imagery, from the basic structure to the fine details. The open-tread stairs, for instance, are patterned after those in nearby windmills and the railings are inspired by wire fencing. The house is located on a knoll, nestled between two existing barns that provide the context and the stylistic reference for the house.

The design springs from Western traditions of barn building. More typically in the Eastern states, says Luchetti, barns and buildings were constructed using a post, beam, and timber framing system. Western barns typically were balloon-framed, often using the "two-by" approach, which means that all the wood is in multiples of two—two-by-fours, two-by-eights, and so forth. The Coyote Valley ranch house follows the latter construction method.

Luchetti grew up in San Francisco, attended the University of California at Berkeley, and then moved east for his architecture degree at the Harvard Graduate School of Design. He stayed on to teach there and ultimately set up his practice in Cambridge, Massachusetts. And though he designed the family house long-distance, he did it for terrain he knew well and loved. He set the house on a sloping knoll, on high ground oriented east and west to capture prevailing breezes, to gain the most natural ventilation and protection from the sun. Large roof overhangs and screened porches also shade the house from the stronger afternoon sun.

He created a single, central gabled "barn" and surrounded it with a series of "sheds" and outdoor spaces. A pergola

The Luchetti Family

reaches uphill to frame a space used for barbecuing and dining, extending the interior living into the natural environment; this outdoor "room" is oriented to the cardinal points of the compass. As a house designed for multiple generations to use for years to come, it has such sophisticated elements as wood ovens and herb beds and such simple amenities as sandboxes and tricycle paths.

Inside, the main living space is divided into three areas—living room, dining room, and television lounge. The kitchen is housed in one of the adjoining sheds, adjacent to the dining room. A freestanding fireplace, open to both rooms, divides the living and dining areas. A screened porch wraps around two sides of the living room and TV lounge, while a large sundeck opens off the dining area. There are two self-contained bedroom suites on the first floor, each with its own bathroom and deck, and two more above, also with a bathroom and a deck. An additional sleeping loft on the second floor accommodates the overflow, when even a modest percentage of this family gathers. The house is designed for a big family flowing through. There are spaces to be together and spaces to be separate. And when Lawrence and Petra Luchetti are alone—seldom and usually by chance—they do not need to use the upstairs rooms.

Robert Luchetti turned to the earth to divine a color palette for the house. He asked his oldest brother, Larry, to gather and send him "moss, grass, leaves, the earth itself, which is dark red—this is a very old part of California, geologically speaking," he says. "I had a box full of colors to work with," Luchetti explains, "sage green, dark green, deep red." Siding is stained board-and-batten along with stained plywood paneling; the roof is galvanized metal. Inside, the colors are more subdued, while the structural elements are left exposed, giving the space a powerful dynamic feeling. "In photographs, it somehow looks high-tech," says Luchetti, "but there's nothing high tech about this house. It's just wood and nails."

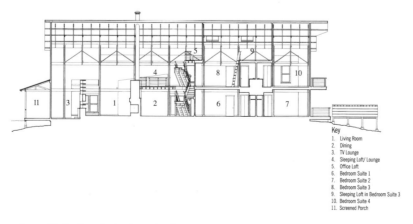

Key
1. Living Room
2. Dining
3. TV Lounge
4. Sleeping Loft/ Lounge
5. Office Loft
6. Bedroom Suite 1
7. Bedroom Suite 2
8. Bedroom Suite 3
9. Sleeping Loft in Bedroom Suite 3
10. Bedroom Suite 4
11. Screened Porch

Plan section shows how the house accommodates a big family gathering for weekends and reunions.

LEFT **Luchetti based the design on barn architecture in the west, a balloon framed structure.**

Natural light through the timber frame and roof skylight

The stairway design incorporates the windmill on the working ranch.

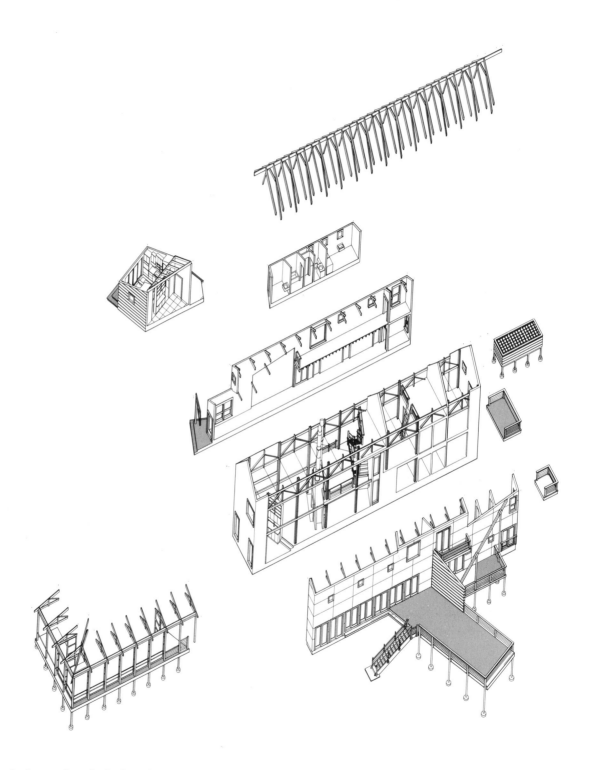

Sections reveal complex framing system.

"Back" of house looks out to Coyote Valley.

MARK AND PETER ANDERSON

Charles and Margaret Anderson House

GIG HARBOR, WASHINGTON 1989–1995

MARK AND PETER ANDERSON GREW UP WORKING WITH WOOD. AS TEENAGERS, THEY HELPED their parents build a cabin on Harstene Island in Puget Sound. Even today, the Anderson brothers work together in an architectural practice that runs the gamut from art to craft; they are at once conceptual artists, designers, and builders.

The family has a long history of "making things," from grandparents, parents, down to the children. Mark and Peter Anderson began with toys and erector sets and graduated to snow forts, sand pits, and tree houses, before going on to real (and bigger) buildings, among them the house they created for their parents. The house was years in the making, starting with the search for a good piece of land. "We had been planning to build a new house for our parents for some time," Peter and Mark Anderson agree, "but I suppose the beginning of the real design work came with finding that particular piece of property."

The land they found was a narrow, south-facing point jutting into Puget Sound with a 180-degree view from Mt. Rainier on the east to the Olympic Mountains on the west. It had been occupied since 1910, and planted over the years: cherry, peach, apple, pear, and plum trees; grape arbors, berry patches (blackberries, blueberries, and huckleberries), and dahlia beds; and divided by a sequence of rock walls. The old bungalow that stood on the site was in deteriorated condition and declining rapidly; Mark and Peter Anderson moved their

LEFT
A house of angles

Left to right, Margaret, Kirsten, Charles, Mark, and Peter Anderson

office there. The first step was to rebuild the dock, then to build a greenhouse at the water's edge and a studio on the inland portion of the property. The studio houses a large workshop downstairs and a small apartment upstairs where Charles and Margaret Anderson

lived while the main house was being built. That was an important step, say the Anderson brothers; by both living on the site and building there, all family members gained an intimate understanding of the place—the slant of the sun, the views to water and mountains, the nuances of ecological life.

The Andersons used the studio design as a "rough draft" for the house, though with less expensive and more rustic materials, yet many of the same features that ultimately found their way into the main building. "This was really a very collaborative project," says Peter Anderson, "with Mark and me and my parents all working together

137
CHARLES AND MARGARET ANDERSON HOUSE

closely throughout the process." The two sons designed while the parents provided a great deal of hands-on labor, making projects that were either time-intensive or sufficiently ill-defined to make a contractor and crew outrageously expensive and ineffective.

The Anderson family numbers five. Kirsten, the eldest, then Mark and Peter. Charles Anderson, a professor of organic chemistry, and Margaret, an administrative assistant, married while he was in graduate school; from the start, even when they had little money, they bought or made furniture and objects of high quality, including an Eames chair and Herman Miller lamps. "I think of my parents as modernists," says Peter Anderson, "not in the sense that they like a particular design style but that they like the design principles of the modern age." Mark and Peter live nearby; Kristen lives in western Massachusetts and travels back home during the year. The whole family spends Christmas together and also gathers at summer's end for a week or more. Family traditions, especially those revolving around Christmas, became essential in shaping the house. The Anderson brothers shaped the living room, for example, by envisioning where family members might sit as well as by the size of Christmas tree that could fit in the space. A black steel krumkakke iron holds a place of honor in the kitchen; it is used to make a Norwegian Christmas cookie, and it has been in Margaret Anderson's family for so many generations that nobody is actually sure how old it is.

The tree column rising in the middle of the living room is another symbolic gesture, though not one directly related to family ritual. The tree is a Port Orford cedar, relatively rare and prized by boat builders for its "beauty and supple strength," says Peter Anderson. The family ultimately decided to cut it down, he says, because "we would appreciate the tree more as a portion of the interior of the house, as the main central support in the main space."

The house is open, with few rooms defined in the traditional way with walls and doors. Charles and Margaret Anderson are there alone most of the time, and Mark and Peter wanted to make it seem intimate. Structurally, the room is composed of three elements, which are "set into and impacted by the complex, contradictory reality of the site." The plan was governed by the legal constraints of shoreline setbacks and natural laws of water runoff. The Andersons also wanted to maintain the site's topography and forestation; thus the house's footprint follows the form of the original bungalow.

The result of all this is a house of angles, put together as a three-dimensional puzzle. In profile, the metal roofs tilt in shed-like fashion. Interior rooms are irregularly shaped. The kitchen is at the center of it all, complete with a granite "egg-shaped" kitchen island, a metaphor for the core of family home.

For windows, Mark and Peter Anderson found an "old-time manufacturer of wooden windows," who sold them the collected accumulations in his warehouse—windows of ages unknown, but aged. "Out of this collection," says Peter, "the ones we chose to use in the house had mostly been built for the restoration of a lodge building at Mt. Rainier National

Park. The buildings there had been a part of our childhood. . . . So in addition to the fact that the windows were beautifully made and we would have liked them anyway, we always have felt a strong family connection to the buildings they were made for." The Anderson brothers had bought the windows before they had even begun designing their parents' house; they continued to study and think about them as they proceeded. The windows became key to the look and feel of the design.

BELOW
Site plan showing placement of house and studio on narrow lot fronting Puget Sound.

The idea of materials that improve with age was also central. The Anderson brothers chose exposed Douglas fir for interior floors, cabinetry, and some paneled walls, an uncommon use for this richly grained softwood. Because Douglas fir dramatically changes in color as it ages and dries, it is generally stained or painted; the Andersons decided to let the aging process continue naturally. Ceilings are hemlock, and bathrooms and the sauna are cedar.

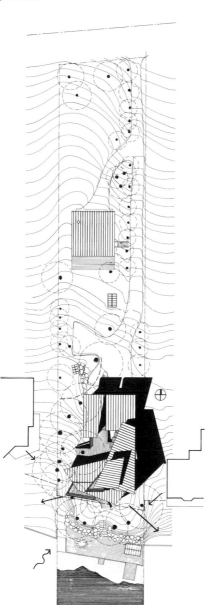

The Andersons oiled all the exposed woods, rather than finishing them with sealants or stains. The carpentry draws on the historic traditions of Arts-and-Crafts furniture-making, using butt joints with square ends. For construction, the family found boat builders and old-time woodworkers. "Other than the kitchen appliances and plumbing fixtures," says Peter Anderson, "there is little in this house to provide clues to when it was built."

The woods are rich and the painted walls are deeply hued, mostly cobalt blue. The carnelian (or mahogany) granite used in the kitchen for counters was a favorite of Charles Anderson's father (Mark's and Peter' grandfather), who was a stone cutter for four decades, carving monuments across Minnesota, South Dakota, and Iowa, from the 1920s on.

This regard for both family and history fills the house. Charles and Margaret Anderson are the two full-time residents, but their three children think of it as theirs as well. "It may sound like a cliché to say that we designed and built this house to last," says Peter Anderson. "But there is a deeper sense of permanence in this house, the idea that it is a permanent part of our family."

The cedar tree column provided a focal point for the design.

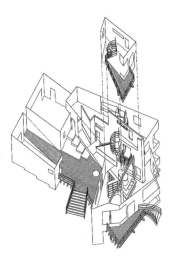

A computer-generated axonometric view of the house elements joined like pieces of a puzzle.

RIGHT The house makes use of decks and balconies for outdoor living spaces.

Richly clad in wood, carefully selected and left to age naturally

RIGHT **The kitchen is central to the Anderson's family and thus opens to the living spaces.**

The house reflects the vernacular architecture of the Sierra Nevada foothills.

CHRIS PARLETTE

Bette Parlette and John Fischer House

JACKSON, CALIFORNIA 1995

CHRIS PARLETTE TOOK HIS CAMERA AND HIS MOTHER AND SET OFF TO STUDY THE BUILDINGS of the Sierra Nevada foothills—barns and shacks and abandoned logging huts. He was enamored of the vernacular architecture of this rugged countryside, once the province of miners, loggers, and grazing sheep. "I wanted to do a house that would maintain the character of this place," he says. Bette Parlette, however, was not convinced, at least at first.

After months of trekking around with her son, Bette Parlette and her new husband, John Fischer, embraced the idea completely. "It really clicked," Chris Parlette says. "They saw the connection and decided to do a house that fit in with the area's history, albeit one in keeping with the budget."

The land Parlette and Fischer owned was a five-acre site that sloped gradually upwards, a rise of 50 feet from a gravel road below. An old dirt logging road divided the site, and the land had been turned over to grazing sheep, who in turn brought in the manzanita grass that in the west grows tall and takes over the entire landscape preventing any small trees from growing.

The house sits on the plateau, and the land beyond falls away to the east and the terrain opens a bit, letting a long view out to the Blue Mountains emerge in the distance. An important first step was to clear out all the brush, leaving the existing trees and introducing new pines that in turn will re-seed, "the making of a new forest," explains Parlette.

Bette Parlette, on site, during construction

For Chris Parlette, a recent graduate of the University of California at Berkeley, the commission was his first independent design. He had completed remodeling jobs on his own and worked as a project manager and senior designer in the firm of Wilson Associates, but this project literally and metaphorically represented "a whole new frontier" for him.

Most new houses in the region, even in the rugged Sierra Nevadas, tend to be what Parlette calls "transplanted stocked-in-Modesto tract houses, just simple boxes with gables." Parlette was not thinking that way; he had long admired the work of San Francisco firm of Fernau & Hartman and carefully studied the way they adapted the vernacular to create new and original buildings. Their methodology became an inspiration.

Parlette served as both designer and construction manager on this house. A high school friend, Chris Chaput, oversaw the daily on-site work, but Parlette spent every weekend and all his vacation weeks on the

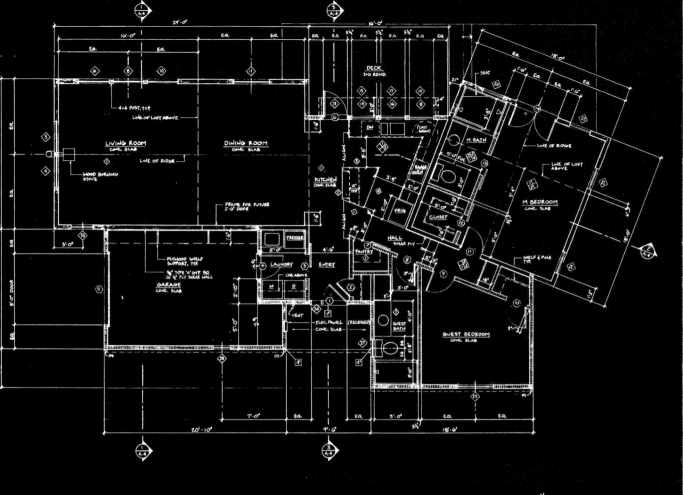

FLOOR PLAN
1/8"=1'-0"

N

job, framing the house, installing windows, building cabinets and trim. During construction, Bette Parlette moved nearby, into what her son calls "a rickety old geodesic dome," to be close at hand when decisions needed to be made.

The house falls into three distinct parts—a living area, a kitchen and utilities area, and the sleeping quarters. The form is essentially two barnlike structures linked by a metal-clad shed that contains the service elements of the house (the kitchen and garage). "Each piece relates in an abstracted way to an older barn structure in the woods," says Parlette. For example, one wall of the kitchen is actually the wood siding of the master bedroom, as if it actually had been a barn with an addition.

Color plays an important role in the design, says Parlette, in part to reinforce the "hierarchical logic of the architecture." The exterior of the living room is a faded gray-green; the bedroom "barn" is a faded tan. On the interior, both the living room and master bedroom are clad in wood, a combination of Douglas fir and pine. The kitchen relies on "a more exuberant array of materials and colors," says Parlette. Cabinets are green, finished in a baked-on painted patina. Multi-colored slate forms both backsplash and window sills. A board-formed concrete kitchen island is topped with a three-inch-thick piece of black concrete in a trapezoidal shape.

The floors, too, are concrete. Parlette didn't cover the slab-on-grade foundation (with radiant heat piped through), but created the finished flooring by applying colored sealants, using different shades to distinguish one part of the house from another. The living room floor is a rusty leather hue, while the bedrooms are an ochre. For the kitchen floor, he used a clear sealant, so that the natural concrete tone is revealed.

To reinforce the rustic sensibilities, Parlette hung sliding plank "barn" doors throughout the house. At one end of the living room is a singular wood stove with a flu pipe that runs up the wall and then outside. Behind it is a piece of steel that was covered with salt water and left outdoors to weather for three weeks; the resulting pattern of rust transforms plain metal into a kind of sculptural piece. Another invention is in the light fixtures, which are custom copper wedges, simple shrouds over a basic bulb. They too were left outside to weather, then Parlette applied a patina to further age them.

All this entered into making a rustic house in the foothills, a house that could go into a photo album of local historic vernacular buildings, but is clearly of its own place and generation.

Plan shows how various pieces of the house work together.

View through living room into kitchen is framed by a loft space.

RIGHT **Kitchen "island" has a base of board-formed concrete topped by a black concrete slab.**

NORTH ELEVATION

Parlette drew a series of studies for volume, massing, and proportion.

RIGHT **The two primary structures of the house are linked by the corrugated metal connector housing the kitchen.**

The house is long and narrow, to take advantage of the site and offer privacy to family members.

DONNA KACMAR

Steve and Diana Kacmar House

CYPRESS COVE, SPRING BRANCH, TEXAS 1993–1997

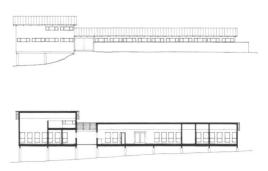

The linear house in section

THE KACMAR FAMILY HAD OWNED THIS LAND FOR MANY YEARS, A SINGLE ACRE IN THE RUGGED
Texas hill country midway between San Antonio and Austin. A picnic table stood on the
site, and the family would head to the hills on Sunday outings. The longstanding plan was
to build a house. Then Donna Kacmar began thinking about this "unbuilt" house as an
architectural undergraduate at Texas A & M University. The design evolved over many
years, and by the time the house was built, Donna Kacmar had a graduate degree and was
an associate in the Houston architectural firm of Natalye Appel as well as an adjunct professor at Rice University and the University of Houston.

"There was a lot of heated debate before [my parents] actually paid me to design the
house—at Thanksgiving, at Christmas—so we really came to very similar points of view,"
says Kacmar. "And even after it was under way, we went over things more than I have with
any client. Every detail was discussed, and faxed back and forth." Donna's sister Cynthia
provided third-party critiques from time to time.

The whole family maintains an avid interest in architecture. Steve Kacmar is a civil
engineer with a passionate interest in design; Diana Kacmar holds a master's in business
administration but went back to school to get a second degree in urban planning. Early on,
while Donna was still an undergraduate, her parents hired an outside architect, but his
design proved unbuildable. And, said Steve and Diana Kacmar, "how could you not use the
architectural skills of your daughter for such a personal project?"

The site the elder Kacmars selected as "a compromise between a thousand-acre ranch
and subdivision" is primarily flat, but the elevation falls off sharply to afford distant views

Steve, Diana, Cynthia, and Donna Kacmar

into the Texas hills. Even though the land itself is modest in size, the site looks out onto a
large holding that is dedicated in perpetuity as ranch land.

Donna Kacmar initially drew one single, long building
with several outbuildings attached. That design eventually
evolved into a house that is essentially a rectangle—a long
and narrow 124 feet by 16 feet—running east and west
along the edge of the drop-off. It is in fact two connected
structures that read as one. The idea was to have a "living
house" and a "work house," says Kacmar, one dwelling
divided into two, part for living and part for working. Even
the view is varied, "sometimes through trees, sometimes
over trees," says Kacmar. The longest, most dramatic views
are to the south.

As a civil engineer, Steve Kacmar is interested in structure and order, and that in many ways propelled the design.
Donna obliged by designing the house along a regular
eight-foot modular system, wood rafters tied together by

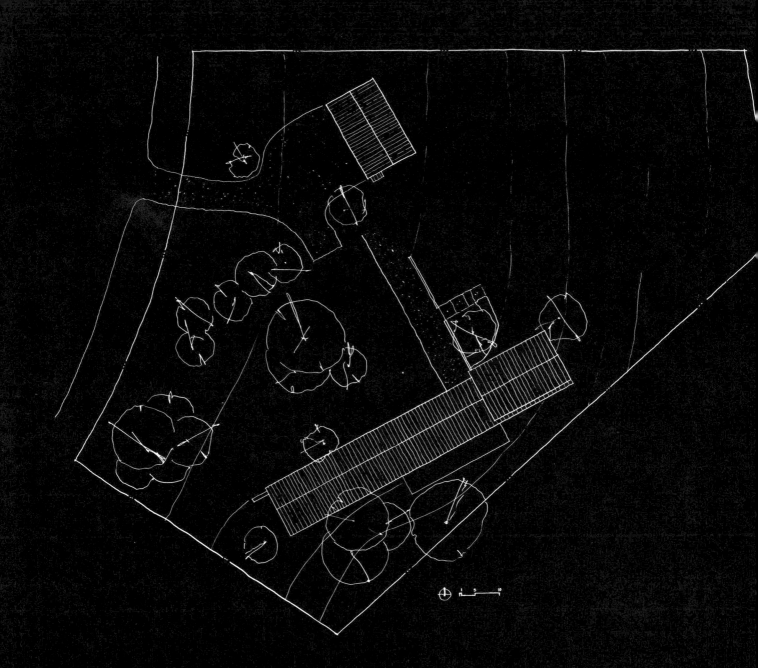

steel rods. "The strategy was to accommodate the view and do it with a rational structural system," she says. A four-foot-wide hallway runs along the "view side" of the house, connecting each of the rooms. "Its a swath that nothing penetrates," says Kacmar.

Though her parents are still some years away from retirement, daughter Donna was mindful of the notion that this would be the house they would live in as they got older. Thus it is on one floor. It is also designed to give its occupants the opportunity to have space between them, a consideration not just for retirement but also significant in rural living where there is no neighborhood.

The house is styled in the regional vernacular to reflect the local condition. The buildings draw on such rural imagery as barns and sheds. The materials include stone from nearby sources and stucco. The design relies on time-tested precepts: windows are set low enough to capture prevailing breezes or high enough to let heat out. The metal roof reflects heat.

Donna selected interior finishes not just for their beauty and durability; Diana Kacmar has chemical intolerances and all woods needed to be natural, not composites. Built-in cabinets are maple, a stable and untreated wood, rather than the more typical formaldehyde-infused plywood. Kacmar's mandate was to find "inert materials, easy to clean and easy to maintain—and if that wasn't enough, also inexpensive." Simplicity became a dominant motif. Floors are oak. Doors are fir.

In many ways, this house represents a return to the family's beginnings as well. The young Kacmars, just starting out, lived for a period in a trailer. Though the Spring Branch house is much bigger, it has an evolutionary relationship with the trailer.

A profound sense of family permeates the whole project. Kacmar knew to let the house sprawl a bit, because hers is a family of individuals who need space. "The house allows for separate activities, separate identities, and yet the big living and dining space allows for the family to gather and even then not be on top of each other," she explains. Its a house for her parents to live in comfortably, alone, and a house for family gatherings.

"Almost every time I'm up there my dad will put his arm around me and walk me through and say 'this is a really great house,'" says Kacmar. "I feel that it isn't my house but ours. It was a real collaborative venture."

Site plan shows entrance at top left corner.

Portions of the house are raised on concrete columns.

Clerestory windows indirectly light the living room

The house separates work and rest spaces, offering opportunities for sociability and quiet.

A strict modular grid governed the design and is apparent even from the spacing of the windows.

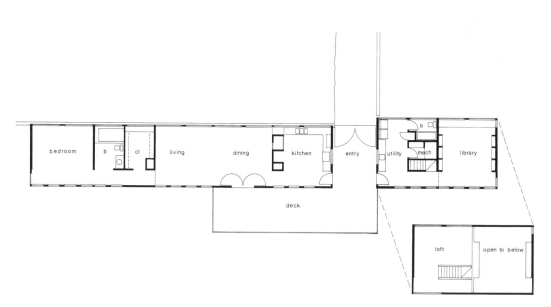

Floor plan showing linear nature of the house.

Leonard and Else Cobb House

SEATTLE, WASHINGTON 1995–1998

ERIC COBB GREW UP IN A DUTCH COLONIAL STYLE HOUSE IN SEATTLE, A HOUSE HE DESCRIBES as being "totally symmetrical with four columns out front." It was this house his parents, Leonard and Else Cobb, asked him to replace. No one in the family held much lingering sentiment for it. "That house never made a very personal impression on anybody. It some-how didn't connect," Eric Cobb says.

What was personal to the family was furniture. Else Cobb, a native of Holland and a sculptor in bronze, had amassed a wide-ranging collection of furniture over the years, from Barcelona chairs to fifteenth-century heirlooms.

Leonard and Else Cobb had initially thought of living in a condominium apartment, then looked at townhouses. The decision to build a house was followed by about a year-and-a-half of search for the site. Land is scarce in Seattle. The lot they settled on is steeply sloped, selected in part for its sun exposure but also for its huge maple trees. "It was a very provocative site but also more challenging than most," Cobb says. "Part of the process was making a house my parents could grow old in, and a steep site certainly isn't ideal."

The Dutch Colonial was sold, and Leonard and Else Cobb moved to a rental house, which "allowed them to dislodge themselves," say Cobb. This was to the architect's advantage, because the house he was designing was radically different from the family's longtime residence.

The site, however, became the generator of the house's form. The hillside meant that the design could take advantage of the many mature trees in the neighborhood, as if the house stood amid a park, rather than in center-city Seattle. Thus, the house is configured to take full advantage of the trees. An important consideration for Cobb was to offer a range of exposures to both sunlight and views, without the simple demarcations of inside and outside

Cobb was educated first at the University of Washington, then received a master's degree at Columbia University. He stayed on in New York to work for Richard Meier, and then Henry Smith-Miller and Laurie Hawkinson. The commission to design a house for his parents gave him the incentive to move back West and to open his own practice. He designed much of this house, however, from a distance, before he returned to Seattle.

LEFT
The house has a strong horizontal quality with bands of windows and sun shields above them.

Else, left, and Leonard Cobb at work during construction.

The design has a modern aesthetic that is rooted in early California modernists such as Richard Neutra. It is horizontal in plan and imparts what Cobb calls the "spirit of expansive space." There are also many modern details—corner glass, flush baseboards, and planar surfaces. "My interest," says Cobb "was to keep the architectural presence as tight and as clean as possible. I didn't want the exterior to be a screaming object statement. Instead I wanted a calm composition. I did want the interior to have a striking spatial presence like the inside of a nautilus shell in which the whole thing opens up with spaces connected and with transparencies between them."

Two different paths lead into the house and back out again. One path is the "domestic path," approached by automobile and looping through the private and practical parts of the house—carport, kitchen, bedroom. The other is the "guest path." It starts on the sidewalk and leads up a short flight of exterior stairs, traverses the front of the house, then ascends a steel stair at the main entry and heads into the living room, "all the more formal open spaces," then up the main stairs to the second floor. Here, on the upper level, the two paths meet and spiral up to the roof deck.

For Cobb, one of the most difficult propositions was getting his parents, long accustomed to tradition-bound houses, to "understand open space and space that wasn't just defined by walls and doors." Then too, each parent responded to the design process and the ongoing project very differently. His mother, the sculptor, could take a plan and turn it into a "beautiful perspective drawing of the space"; his father, a retired physician, could see the project in more functional terms. "He's digital," says Cobb, "He thinks in terms of spread sheets."

Initially, he wasn't sure how his parents would respond to the idea of a modern house, but he persuaded them, by word and deed, that modernism "need not be seen as the severe and destructive thing it was in the late '60s." He bought them Le Corbusier's book, *La Petite Maison,* which documents the Swiss architect's design for his mother on Lake Geneva, a gentle little house. Cobb thought it would offer subtle messages to his parents that their house could have a presence on its site, not simply be an object of modernism.

Together, they focused their design discussions on the furniture that had filled the Dutch Colonial house. For the senior Cobbs, it was familiar, tangible, and visual. Eric Cobb developed computer models of chairs, sofas, tables, even rugs to show how they would fit in the space and vice versa. He showed how the space he was designing embraced their belongings. Another goal was to make each of the rooms useful, to make the most of a smaller space than they had lived in before.

As construction began, the senior Cobbs became informal construction foremen. At one point, however, after the house was framed, Leonard Cobb realized that it was missing a laundry chute and, to his mind, every house must have a laundry chute. "I said that I'd do it," says the architect, "but he had to let me do it without constraints on the design." Thus a stainless steel tube with a lid was placed in the master bathroom, directly opposite the toilet. "To this day, he says it's one of the best parts of the house."

From the start, Leonard and Else Cobb had asked for two things: cedar siding on the exterior and hardwood floors within. The house has both (though the senior Cobbs expected dark floors rather than the paler maple their son chose) along with white walls and a trim stone that is blue with a natural cleft finish. "It is a very limited material palette," says Cobb. For Leonard and Else Cobb, an awareness of the architect's craft grew in the course of construction. After they had moved in, they continued to discover aspects of the design, such as glass corners and wide open vistas. "The very loose vocabulary of geometries afforded opportunities for many more unusual and personal moments in this house." And ironically enough, Else and Leonard Cobb feel that it is this house—with its greater abstraction—that feels more like a home, than the more traditional one of Eric Cobb's youth. "Ultimately, I just can't say enough about their willingness to experiment," concludes Cobb. "No one knew exactly where we were going with this, but they showed no fear."

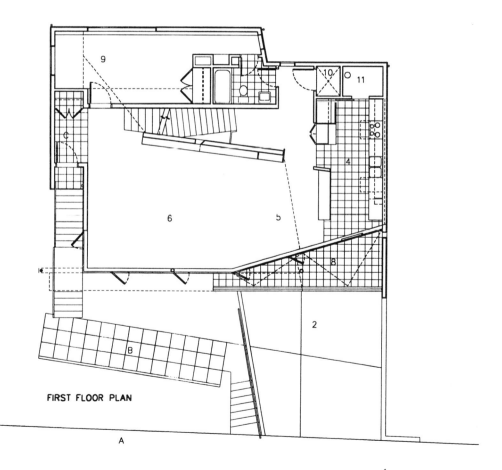

FIRST FLOOR PLAN

A plan with many exposures to light and views

The house had to fit onto a tight wooded lot in a built-up Seattle neighborhood.

A living room designed to fit the Cobb's collection of fine furniture.

RIGHT **Stairways both separate and connect public and private portions of the house.**

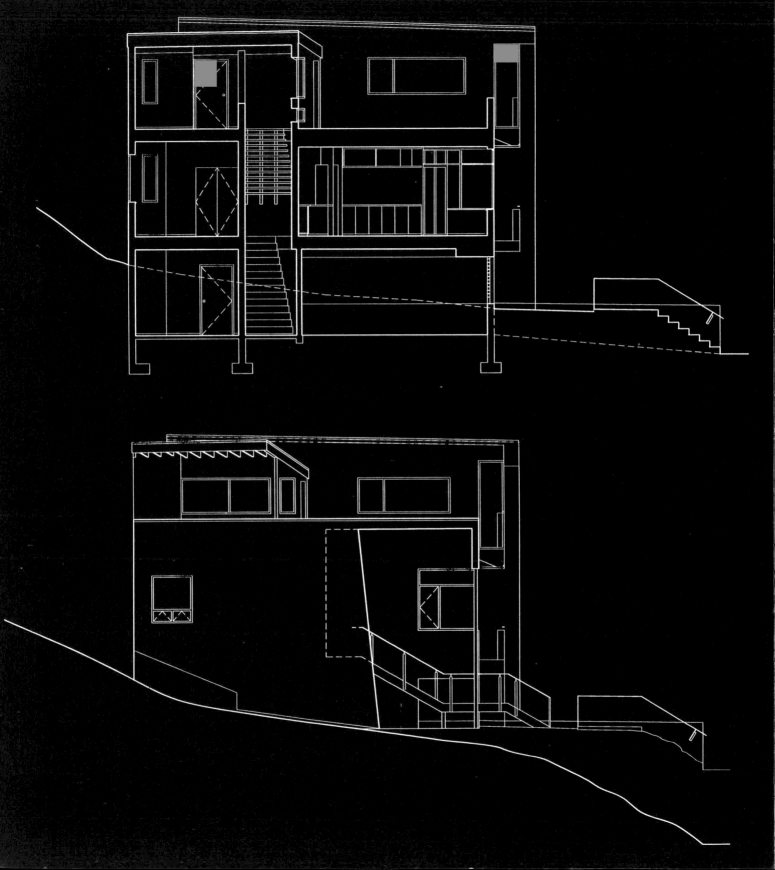

Glass corners, connecting spaces, and transparencies

LEFT A complex set of "paths" governs the circulation to and through the house.

The Larson house is definitely a "lake house," not a transplanted suburban manse.

MARK AND JEAN LARSON

David and Kathryn Larson House

LAKE SYLVIA, MINNESOTA 1997

MARK AND JEAN LARSON DISCOVERED MIDWAY THROUGH THE DESIGN OF THIS LAKE HOUSE FOR David and Kathryn Larson, Mark's parents, that they were expecting a baby. They decided to announce it this way: they tucked a tiny crib into one of the bedrooms in the scale model and took it to a review session. Toward the end of the session, Kathryn Larson noticed the miniscule baby bed. "A crib?" she asked. "A crib. . . . A crib!"

Ironically, the baby's due date was exactly the scheduled completion day for the lake house. But as these things go, Andrew Larson arrived two months early and the house delivered four months late.

Like many Minnesotans, the Larson family had a long tradition of "going to the lake." Mark Larson's grandfather owned a cottage that became the gathering place for the whole family. David and Kathryn Larson bought their own small pine cabin on a peninsula between Twin Lake and Lake Sylvia near Annandale 18 years ago. It was small and it was not winterized. At first, when Mark and Jean Larson were still architecture students at the University of Minnesota, the senior Larsons thought they would renovate, adding a deck and heat and insulation to protect the little house against the subzero temperatures and biting winds of Minnesota winters. That turned out to be too much work. It required digging frost footings 42 inches into the ground; replacing all the single-pane windows with double panes; pulling off the walls and the roof to insulate and rebuild. The Larsons—David, Kathryn, Mark, and Jean—decided it was just not worth it.

The Larsons finally concluded that there was only one way to go: tear down and build anew. Still, they came to that decision with a fair amount of remorse, so they looked for continuity. Ultimately they decided to salvage what they could from the old house and reuse it in the new one.

Jean and Mark Larson on site

"My parents felt it was kind of a decadent thing to do, to tear down the cabin," says Mark Larson. "One of the reasons they grew to feel comfortable was that we were salvaging as much as we could." Old windows went to the "bunkhouse," which has become the overflow sleeping quarters for summer guests. The original timbers became beams in the new, thus defining the house's structural proportions. The old timbers, says Mark Larson, "really defined the shape of the house."

By the time construction was underway, the Larsons (he works at Hammel Green & Abrahamson and she at Susanka Mulhady & Partners) had put more than six years into the project. They were architectural classmates at the University of Minnesota, but the two (life) partners had not actually collaborated on a design before.

The house intentionally reflects the family's Scandinavian heritage. That David Larson is of Norwegian descent affected not just the product but the process. Mark Larson notes that his parents did not rush to judgment on any

All the living spaces open onto one another.

step of the design, which was good but also frustrating to the young designers who yearned for instant feedback. "My parents were very slow and careful about their decision making. I think that their maturity is in the building, which is nice. I feel more comfortable knowing that they thought everything through, but at the time it was often hard to get responses." He is careful to add, "of course I know them well, and now better than ever." The senior Larsons also needed to see a lot of detail during the design process. "We did a lot of drawings, schemes, models," says Mark Larson. "My father would look at it and squint. He had to have the time to think about it and would not just blurt out anything. Two weeks later, they'd come back and say, 'this is the direction we want to follow.'"

Aesthetically, the Norwegian influence comes through in a number of ways—in the sturdy, almost stoic, cabin-like quality of the house; in the clean, somewhat conservative and fairly modern approach to the design, coupled with the use of lots of wood, warmer materials and deep colors. "Norwegians are not afraid of color" says Larson. The house is clad in a rustic cedar, cut in a horizontal tongue-and-groove. It has a dark green metal roof and a deep red stucco base.

The main level relies on an open floor plan, which means that the living and dining spaces flow one into the other; a stone fireplace sits at one end of the living room; at the other end is a coal-burning stove. The open living room rises to a vaulted ceiling, framed by a clear glass-paned window wall that looks out onto wide-open lake views. The house is nestled into a hillside, with the service areas tucked in back.

Upstairs, the bedrooms are small, kept so to reinforce the idea that this is a weekend and summer place and not a transplanted suburban residence. The bedroom closets are "locker-sized," says Mark Larson, "with just room enough for a couple of duffel bags." Another cabin-like feature is the lack of insulated space between the downstairs ceiling and the upstairs bedrooms: only the structural supports, which make it noisy, to say the least.

Throughout, black metal dominates details: painted handrails, steel beam supports, the woodburning stove. Slate blocks edge each of the entryways, to capture snow and dirt and autumn leaves as family members enter the house. The fireplace includes large stones David and Kathryn collected to commemorate the family's past. One, for example, comes from the foundation of the house in which David Larson grew up; another from the homestead that Kathryn Larson's family has farmed for many generations. "There's a sense of nostalgia here," says Mark Larson. "We can look up and still see the old finish on the beams. The house feels like it's been here more than two years."

The living room fireplace made of stones that connect to the family's past

RIGHT Timber from the family's old lake cottage was re-used in the ﬂ

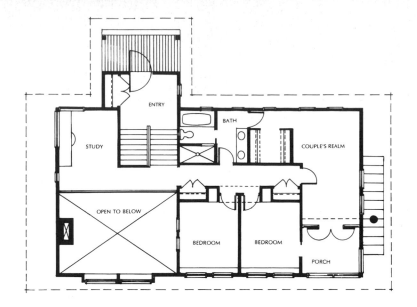

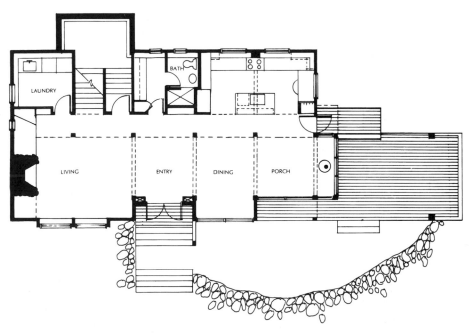

First-floor plan, bottom, and second-floor plan, top

RIGHT **A coal-burning stove balances out the fireplace at the other end of the open living room.**

Rocci and Anne Lombard House

FORT LAUDERDALE, FLORIDA 1998

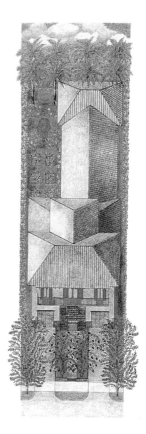

ONLY ONE NARROW LOT REMAINED IN THIS PRIME WATERFRONT neighborhood built in the 1920's as a planned garden "suburb" of Fort Lauderdale. It was on this site that Joanna Lombard and Denis Hector built the house for Anne and Rocci Lombard, known as Clematis House.

It is a "sideyard" house in a garden setting, and it is intended to conjure up associations with the literary idea of paradise. The house is named for the street it sits on, Clematis Street, though ironically the clematis vine does not grow in south Florida, even while numerous native and exotic flowering trees and vines bloom in the neighborhood.

The neighborhood is built on a peninsula—bounded by the Intracoastal Waterway, the New River, and Sunset Lake—formed by the ridges of native oolitic limestone and shifting fill. It aligns with the Atlantic Ocean, less than a mile to the east.

TOP RIGHT
Pencil drawing of the house's garden paradise.

LEFT
The two-story living room with high clerestory windows opens out onto an open loggia.

Denis Hector, Rocci, Anne, and Joanna Lombard, left to right

Rocci and Anne Lombard had been living in a rather capacious house with a view of the Intracoastal Waterway. The house dated to the 1950s and had rooms that offered lots of space but little grace; there were few walls for paintings and no good places to arrange furniture for comfortable conversation. In turn, intimacy and personal connectedness were two goals in this design.

The architects, married to one another and associate professors at the University of Miami School of Architecture (she is a Tulane- and Harvard-educated architect and garden scholar who runs the first-year program, and he, with degrees from Cornell and the University of Pennsylvania, is a structures expert and the school's director of graduate studies) are also parents of two young children. Thus, this was conceived as a house for three generations to enjoy, with a second-floor retreat and playroom for visiting grandchildren.

Another goal was to meet the neighborhood with the face of a villa, while still providing a private retreat in the contained garden. "The architectural language," says Joanna Lombard, "refers to the origins of the city and the qualities of light and landscape unique to this particular place."

Lombard and Hector took the form of the house from eighteenth- and nineteenth-century architectural prototypes, particularly from houses found in Southeastern towns where land has always been scarce. They designed it with an eye to the environmental sensibility of pioneer houses in the tropics. Thus there are opportunities for heat to rise and for air to flow through the house. It is shielded from the fierce sun but not from the bright light. The plan recalls Fort Lauderdale's pioneer houses: one room deep and lined with verandas. A second-floor balcony facing the street looks out over the tree canopy to a distant glimpse of the Atlantic Ocean.

The house is painted a bold Tuscan yellow, a color that, Joanna Lombard says, "in the early morning sky and in the violet storm light . . . has enough intensity and reflectivity to maintain the glow of rising light." Eaves and ceilings are painted "the aqua of the underside of the clouds, reflections of the sea." Shutters are painted in a traditional Italian garden hue of dark green. An allée of crape myrtles lining the walkway bloom to bright magenta and further set off the bold colors.

Lombard and Hector chose to merge two traditional building techniques in this house—concrete masonry for walls and wood for the roof members, the joinery, and trim. The metal roof reflects another tradition common to Southern and tropical houses. The sequence of rooms inside is an orderly one—living room, kitchen (opening onto one of two small garage spaces), dining room, office, and bedroom. The rooms all look out onto the

A "sideyard" house in a garden setting

JOHANNA LOMBARD AND DENIS HECTOR

long narrow interior covered porch typical of a sideyard plan; the porch, in turn, opens onto a sequence of fragrant gardens, rounds of gardenias off the master bedroom, roses across from the living and dining rooms.

Generational differences are respected here. The master bedroom is in the back of the house, shielded from neighborhood noise. Two bedrooms and a small sitting room/playroom for visiting children and grandchildren are upstairs, overlooking the street. "It is thought out," says Lombard, "so that children and adults intersect by choice, not so much by chance." The porch is a particular asset in this: it is where children can go to be noisy, or, if the children are in the house, adults can find a more serene environment.

At the center of the architectural idea, however, is the notion of nurturing and protecting familial relationships. The two-story living room is compact enough for conversation and intended to be warm and intimate. The dining room opens onto the garden, as do the office, the master bedroom, and the garage workshop. Indeed, the long porch is essentially another room, and though the outdoor area is comparatively small, Rocci and Anne Lombard find themselves using it more than they ever did a previous larger yard.

Joanna Lombard looks at the house and realizes that its design stems partly from the professional interests she and her husband share, both the traditional construction and traditional home-making in the purest sense. It also springs from a deep commitment to family life. "When you are designing a house for your parents, you know their life pretty intimately, and you can be straight and honest," Joanna Lombard explains. "And in that respect, any polemical architectural statements become far less important than simply making a place of comfort."

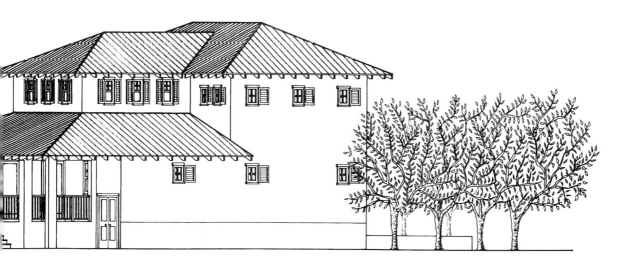

Two views of the Charleston-inspired sideyard house, with porch and small formal gardens.

LEFT The dining room opens out onto the porch, which in turn opens onto a garden.

Architectural details reflect the historic vernacular of southeastern U.S.

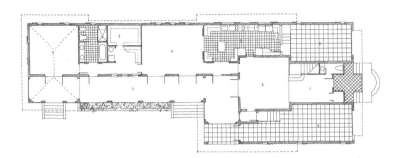

First floor plan shows sequence of rooms from public to private.

RIGHT Stairs lead to the "grandchildren's suite," two bedrooms and a sitting/play area.

Aerial view shows house wrapped around the courtyard.

HENRY MYERBERG

Alvin and Louise Myerberg House

OWINGS MILLS, MARYLAND 1998

English settlers to the region decided to build a version of a Federalist house around the time of the American Revolution. They chose a site deep in the woods and built a well-proportioned and simple two-story home. . . . It was rumored that the site was once sacred to the woodland Indians. They also needed stables which would be convenient to the front door. Time passed and the family grew and subsequent generations added wings to the house. They loved the wooded setting and enjoyed their privacy. Meantime, other neighboring families built homes which began to encroach on their visual domain. In response, later winged additions were built to form a courtyard and connected the house to the stables, which were converted to a garage for autos. During the excavation work in the courtyard, the owners discovered that the courtyard was in fact the outdoor kitchen of the native Americans many hundreds of years ago.

—HENRY MYERBERG to ALVIN and LOUISE MYERBERG, February 5, 1997

Actually, Henry Myerberg made up this story, start to finish. He wanted to give the house he was designing for his parents a historical and regional context, so he devised a narrative underpinning for a house with a past, even though it really did not have one.

Alvin Myerberg, a retired homebuilder, had constructed the house in which Henry had spent much of his childhood; it was built in 1952 when the architect was two. Later the senior Myerbergs, with their children grown and gone, moved to a condominium but they then decided they really wanted to live in a house after all. An added incentive, of course, was their son the architect, educated at the University of Pennsylvania and Harvard's Graduate School of Design, could now design and build a house for them.

Henry, Alvin and Louise Myerberg

There was one very personal issue too. Louise Myerberg has multiple sclerosis. A one-story house tailored to her condition would also allow her access to the outdoors. The Myerbergs found a two-acre site at the end of a long road in a new suburban development in Owings Mills, a town outside of Baltimore built up in the mid-1980s. That is where the fictional history begins.

"I wanted it to seem as if the house stood on a site where the land around it had been sold off over time," Myerberg explains. Thus he designed a "stripped Colonial married to a traditional Maryland country farmhouse, combined with an Annapolis house—kind of an original estate with wings, which look like they've been added over time." It is a brick-faced house with wooden windows painted white and a black slate roof. The materials are as traditional and authentic as could be done given the times. It is, essentially, a one-story house, with just two guest bedrooms on the second floor.

The building process was shaped by the family's various vocations. Because Alvin Myerberg (and his father before him) had been a homebuilder, he had any number of tradesmen to call on. For his new house, he brought back his now 70-plus-year-old superintendent, mason, and electrician. All, of course, are retired "so their sons did the work," says Myerberg. The fathers sat at the site, in lawn chairs, and "supervised."

The interior accommodates the family's eclectic assemblage of furniture and to showcase Alvin and Louise Myerberg's art collection. Finishes are fairly traditional, primarily plaster and paint. The foyer is wood-paneled. The living room fireplace is faced in stone.

The house is laid out in a square shape; the kitchen, living room, and master bedroom each open onto the brick-paved courtyard. Two bedrooms complete the square, and a fourth bedroom upstairs affords space for future live-in help as well as visiting children and grandchildren. And while it is fully handicapped-accessible, the house does not baldly present that fact. Halls and doors are wide to allow for easy passage and the entrance from the garage to the house is ramped for wheelchair use; interior detailing complements the farmhouse and neocolonial architecture. Most important for the couple who occupy the residence, says Henry Myerberg, "the home satisfies their particular lifestyle. . . . The house is mostly about the experience of one-story living."

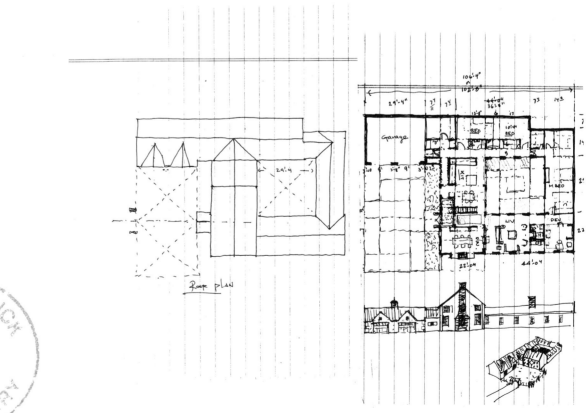

Early sketches showing both ideas behind the house and the way it would be lived in.

The house stands in a suburban neighborhood, yet siting and setting make it seem rural.

Louise and Henry Myerberg at the house's front entrance

The living room accommodates family furniture and the Myerberg's art collection.